The Corporate Overlords will be Kind

Campaign Finance, Representation and Corporate-led Democracy

Radu George Dumitrescu

University of Bucharest, Romania

Series in Politics

VERNON PRESS

www.vernonpress.com

In the Americas:	*In the rest of the world:*
Vernon Press	Vernon Press
1000 N West Street, Suite 1200	C/Sancti Espiritu 17,
Wilmington, Delaware, 19801	Malaga, 29006
United States	Spain

Series in Politics

Library of Congress Control Number: 2021933967

ISBN: 978-1-64889-306-3

Also available: 978-1-62273-879-3 [Hardback]; 978-1-64889-263-9 [PDF, E-Book]

Table of Contents

Abstract		v
Introduction		vii
Chapter I	**The Company – Origins**	1
Chapter II	**The Ruling**	5
Chapter III	**Corporatist Theories**	15
Chapter IV	**The Drafting of a False History**	21
Chapter V	**Citizenship and the Corporation**	25
Chapter VI	**Political Personhood**	37
Chapter VII	**Parties, Corporations and Representation**	41
Chapter VIII	**Partisan Industries and Campaign Contributions**	47
Chapter IX	**Progressive Corporations**	53
	1. Corporations and Women's Day	55
	2. Corporations and Race	57
	3. Gillette and Toxic Masculinity	58
	4. Corporations and Morality	60
	5. Barilla and LGBTQ inclusion	62
	6. Chick-fil-A and Christianity	63
	7. Target, Best Buy and consumer boycotts	65
	8. Corporations and gun-ownership	68
	9. Corporations and the Parkland Shooting	72
	10. Uber & Lyft and the Muslim Ban	75
	11. Airbnb and the West Bank	77
	12. Tiffany's and Transparency	78

13. Nike, Colin Kaepernick and the right to protest   79

14. Corporations and abortion   83

15. Danone and Social Responsibility   85

16. Peloton and Sexism   87

Outcomes   88

Chapter X   **Free Speech and Corporations**   91

Chapter XI   **Trump vs. Corporations**   97

Chapter XII   **China vs. Corporations**   103

Conclusion   113

Bibliography   119

Legal Documents   132

Index   133

Abstract

The following book delves into a developing reality, that of politically-conscious and active companies and corporations,[1] one that has been only recently signaled by the United States Supreme Court ruling in the case *Citizens United v. Federal Election Committee* of 2010. The hypothesis which it proposes is that corporations, from their primary role as economic agents and producers of goods and services, have also developed a role as representatives of their consumers in political and social debates. In issuing ads and statements of support or condemnation of policies, in addition to the more traditional financing of political campaigns and lobbying, corporations gain a heavy political role in society – while still operating as rational and self-interested economic actors – as representatives of their current and future customers and consumers. The magnitude of the change is of such importance and the transformations so great that a new adjective must be added to democracy, and the concept of *corporate-led democracy* can thus be born.

By following their own interest as true utility maximizers, these corporations and companies shape the market to be not only economic, but also political. They prove to be better representatives than the politicians and elected officials that have existed in any political system due to the immediate connection they have with their consumers, which have taken over the ability of the electorate to advance complaints and address social and political issues. Through their day-to-day consumption, people can immediately and significantly impact the new political scene without having to wait entire years for the next election, making corporations, who face a constant and strong competition and so wish to preserve and expand their consumer base, more responsive to their desires, unlike the elected representatives shielded by gerrymandered districts and long mandates. In turn, corporations can be more efficient citizens when laying claims before the state and its officials. This entire process has been going on in the United States primarily in the recent years, and has gone largely unnoticed or ignored by the traditional political science literature.

---

[1] The two terms are used largely interchangeably for the purposes of this book, as both "companies" and "corporations" incorporate individuals as shareholders in a profit-seeking venture. The object of study, however, is the large, multinational corporation that operates on an international stage and is able to exert pressure on state institutions, promote ads before millions of individual consumers and has an established position and reputation within the globalized market. Small-to-medium companies, as such, are not of particular interest in the present book.

The book is structured as follows: chapter I recounts the history of the company, from Sumer to Apple, and the way in which businesses evolved and escaped from under the authority of the state, changing together with the world. Chapter II will detail the *Citizens United* decision in itself, citing the opinions of the majority and the minority of the justices on the Supreme Court regarding it. Chapter III will study the theories which governed the existence and functioning of the corporations in the past. Chapter IV will present the arguments of the critics of the *Citizens United* decision and their recount of how a clerical error started the entire story. Chapter V will visit the theory which connects corporations to the concept of citizenship in an effort to explain their political dimension. The same chapter also looks at the theory of "shareholder democracy," which posits that corporations can represent those who hold shares in them, and thus provide a safeguard against extremism. Chapter VI makes the next logical step from the *Citizens United* ruling and asks what it means to be a person. Chapter VII introduces a new version of representation – not of voters, but of consumers, a system in which the voter loses all importance and where corporations, not politicians or parties, act as representatives. Chapter VIII shows how corporations impact the political system of the United States through campaign contributions and lobbying. Chapter IX presents 16 cases in which well-known corporations took active, partisan stances regarding issues such as sexism, racism, the inclusion of sexual minorities, gun violence, police brutality and so on. Chapter X returns to the core issue of the *Citizens United* ruling, namely that of free speech, presenting how corporations such as Facebook and Twitter have become regulators of speech. Chapter XI visits the relationship between elected officials or politicians and the new politically-awaken corporations by taking US president Donald Trump as the representative of the former. Conversely, Chapter XII shows how corporations fare in the domain of the Chinese government, the guardian of a consumer base that is on the rise. Finally, the last chapter will draw conclusions.

Introduction

In Sidney Lumet's 1976 satirical film *Network*, a news anchor named Howard Beale goes mad.

Beale goes on the air and announces that he will commit suicide. His reason – the world has become corrupted beyond repair by corporate interests set to control and manipulate viewers and consumers in order to rack up profits. Free will is dead, says Beale, and getting angry is the first step toward solving the problem. Captivated by his honest rant against any and all, people tune in to Beale's show in increasing numbers. His bosses and supervisors, noticing the sudden rise in ratings during the news anchor's outburst, disregard their first impulse – that of firing him. Instead, they offer him his own slot as part of an entertainment program and the liberty to continue spreading his rebellious message. On new heights of popularity due to the program, however, Beale tries to interfere with the purchasing of the network by a larger business conglomerate, prompting a meeting with the network's chairman, a man named Jensen, who goes on his own tirade in front of Beale. It is during this discussion – or rather monologue – that the news anchor-turned-prophet gets a glimpse of the truth, forcefully fed to him by the stereotypical corporate man, the avatar of the system.

And so, in a dark room meant for board meetings, the essence of corporate decision-making, Jensen explains to a speechless Beale that he, the truth-telling rebel, is nothing but "an old man who thinks in terms of nations and peoples." "There are no nations," proclaims Jensen. "There are no peoples! There are no Russians! There are no Arabs! There are no Third Worlds! There is no West! There is only one holistic system of systems, one vast and immense, interwoven and interacting, multivariate, multinational dominion of dollars, petro-dollars, electro-dollars, multi-dollars, Reich marks, rubles, pounds and shekels. [...] There is no America. There is no democracy. There is only IBM and ITT and AT&T and DuPont, Dow, Union Carbide and Exxon. Those are the nations of the world today. The world is a collage of corporations inexorably determined by the immutable bylaws of business. The world is a business, Mr. Beale. It has been since man has crawled out of the slime."[1]

The verbal explosion and exposition given by the network chairman, set in a movie from almost half a century ago, turned out to be prophetic. Far from

---

[1] Paddy Chayefsky, *Network*, DVD. Directed by Sidney Lumet, Metro-Goldwyn-Mayer, U.S.A., New York, 1976.

movie sets and fictional realities, the "college of corporations" active on a global scale today has obtained in the US, through the United States Supreme Court case *Citizens United v. Federal Election Committee*, the freedom of speech – of political speech, no less. In 2010, the Court decided that corporations speak through the money they give not to the candidates and parties directly, but to political action committees (PACs), but also through ads and press statements regarding government policy or public political debates.

The corporation is today a free person, able to express opinions about legalizing marijuana, banning assault rifles, setting limits on abortion and so forth. Moreover, it is legally able to finance those with whom it agrees and to attack those with whom it doesn't. The corporation does not die – not like an individual, anyway – and can travel freely through the globalized world. However, with the *Citizens United* decision, waves of criticism coming from left-leaning politicians, activists and other public figures clashed against the shores of the Supreme Court. Most of the complaints regarded the uneven power dynamic between a corporation and an individual. If the former is of one opinion, then the latter, even joined by large numbers of his or her peers, can hardly hope to counterbalance or overpower it. Logically, then, a super-citizen is created, one that does not die, grow old, marry or get sick, who is not bound by borders, and one whose opinions are louder than the voice of other citizens through its finances and influence. The existence of such a *corporate citizen* goes against the democratic logic of equality in a most obvious way.

The debates surrounding the 2010 decision of the Supreme Court also harked back to the foundational topics – what does it mean to be a citizen? Is a separation between "natural" persons – i.e. humans – and "artificial" persons legitimate? What does giving free speech to corporations mean for individual voters?

Questions even went as far back as to revisit the nature of the company. Those who looked discovered Ronald Coase's argument of transactional costs. In 1932, Coase published his article *The Nature of the Firm*. According to Coase, companies existed and succeeded on the market because they lowered the costs of transactions. Individual buyers and sellers would face increased costs of transaction, he argued, were it not for their organizing into companies.[2] But why would corporations, profit-seeking advents by nature, turn to the political sphere? And even more worryingly, how would citizens and individuals take part in a democracy on par with the powerful corporations, if dollars count as

---

[2] Ronald Coase, "The Nature of the Firm," Economica 4, 16 (November 1937): pp. 386-405 https://doi.org/10.1111/j.1468-0335.1937.tb00002.x.

speech and if any given corporation can "speak" volumes, compared to a single individual?

The answer is simple, even if less clear – in such a world, voters and traditional political activists, including parties, lose almost all social and political relevance, while the consumers and corporations gain it all. That is because of several reasons. Firstly, modern-day markets are saturated with virtually indistinguishable goods. Smartphones, for example, have become so complex and diverse that navigating all the options in order to arrive at a suitable phone requires days of research and comparison. Numerous smartphones produced by different companies have only the brand to separate them, and many more are only marginally different from one another. Rationally, from a purely economic standpoint, which is the standpoint one traditionally uses when making a purchase, there is no reason to prefer a smartphone from company X to one produced by company Y, if the price and the features they offer are the same. The choice, then, is left to the – possibly irrational – personal preference of the individual buyer. Some prefer a phone of a certain color, others are faithful to a specific brand and believe its products to be of superior quality because of it, and others still are nonchalantly guided by convenience and purchase whatever smartphone they chance upon in a store or one that is recommended to them by the store clerk. Simply put, the supply matches and even surpasses demand not only in quantity but also in terms of diversity and quality. In economics, this is called a *buyers' market*. The economic power of consumers within a market economy rich with competition has been highlighted by some of the classical advocates of capitalism – Ludwig von Mises, for example. In such a situation, it is the consumers who provide the leading indications within the market, while entrepreneurs and corporations have to put themselves in the consumers' service – even more diligently and eagerly than before – in order to satisfy their own drive for profit and outsell their numerous competitors. This, one can conclude, is capitalism at its best, satisfying needs and having to do it cheaply.

The same Mises says that that the market economy can be viewed as a "democracy of consumers," as it is based on a "daily plebiscite" of the consumers' wishes, in which money spent represents one's opinion in a fashion similar to that of a vote.[3] It is here that one can discover the answer to the question posed by the corporate super-citizens created by the *Citizens United* ruling – will the corporate overlords be ruthless, or will they be kind? Will they

---

[3] Ludwig von Mises, *Interventionism: An Economic Analysis* (Indianopolis: Liberty Fund, 2012).

slash wages, extend working hours, produce low quality goods and undo regulations, or will they be something else?

The present book brings a series of novelties into discussion, enlisting very recent cases in which corporations have *spoken* in the public square. As of now, the debate regarding the involvement of corporations in political and public life has been theorized – although it has never reached the mainstream, remaining bound to notions of corporate social responsibility (CSR) or citizenship. Such interpretations severely limit the scope of the research and fail to grasp the magnitude of the shift that such an involvement brings. Stepping ahead of the theory, the book presents actual instances in which corporations flung themselves into the political agora alongside citizens and governments, not through mere statements and promises but through money, ads and controversial positions.

As the title of this book suggests, the empowered and politically-active corporations will, however, necessarily be kind, tamed by the very environment in which they operate, and will be guided by the wishes and values of the consumer-citizens. At the moment, the daily plebiscite of the market spelled out by Mises has obtained plainly political overtones, as corporations have engulfed significant parts of political representation, on one side, and policy-making powers, on the other. Today, corporations set themselves and their products apart from their competitors through the *values* they profess, not the prices they offer, nor the quality of the goods they sell, and have well-known and proven influence over legislation and government policy. Thus, the corporation represents and legislates.

In order to reach the present reality, one which is still obscured by outdated economic and political theories, corporations have had to go through several theoretical stages in their existence, which chapter III will detail. Before that, however, the story of the corporation must start as any story does – at the beginning.

Chapter I

The Company – Origins

Before IBM and ITT and AT&T, and well before Amazon or Apple, a different kind of corporations took shape. Contemporary society takes the existence of companies and corporations and the products and services they provide at our convenience for granted, but their birth was an undeniable organizational revolution – one comparable to the emergence of the state – that, among others, allowed Western Europe and North America to charge ahead of all other regions of the globe. In their 2003 book *The Company: A Short History of a Revolutionary Idea*, John Micklethwait and Adrian Wooldridge, editors for *The Economist*, trace the evolution of the company from the ancient Sumer to today, noting the various twists and turns that economic activity had gone through under the social and political settings of the age until it reached Ronald Coase's logical efficiency.

While today the corporation exists in a seemingly natural and symbiotic dichotomy with the family, the only other setting and institution which occupies the lives of individuals to a similar extent, the two were closely linked together at the emergence of the former. In ancient Mesopotamia, the right to property was barely formalized by the rich merchant families. The first commercial advents emerged organically out of the family, using family members as its pillars. In Rome, organizations called *societas* collected taxes and grew with the empire, distributing *shares* between partners while the organization's day-to-day activities were run by a *magister*. Without free competition, size was already becoming a problem for the ancient businesses. In ancient China, state-granted monopolies were administered by hereditary bureaucracies. Between the 9th and 12th centuries, the independent merchant cities of present-day Italy also chose family-ran consortiums to operate trade fleets and banks. Trust was scant in a world that offered little security, and the family was one of the few places in which it could be found. Later on, during the Middle Ages, Roman and canonic legislation gradually recognized "corporative persons" like cities, universities or guilds – which proved to be an annoyance to the crown, as they never died or married and thus could not be subjected to the feudal tax.

With the dawn of the modern age, European governments and merchants banded together to found companies with the goal of sacking the resources of the New World and India. Still monopolies of trade, these companies got to have enormous political power. The Honourable East India Trading Company (HEIC), for example, was Great Britain's main tool in administering India.[1] At its peak, it provided almost half of England's trade and oversaw a vast terriority with the help of its immense native army. In India, the HEIC, led by Robert Clive – or Clive of India – started collecting taxes and asserting direct control over parts of the country, acting as an empire within an empire. By 1773, the company also received monopoly rights over the tea trade in America, indirectly prompting the Boston Tea Party.

At the same time, consumers of the age started having their voices heard as well. In 1790, Elizabeth Heyrick launched the first consumer boycott ever, pleading to the citizens of her native Leicester to stop buying "bloody" sugar from the West Indies. Due to her protests, the HEIC was forced to stop buying sugar from the slave plantations and to turn to Bengal for it, as there were no slaves used in the farms there.[2] For the first time in history and indicative of the age to come, the consumers managed to bend to their will the largest company of the day, one which managed territories the size of an empire and held an army on retainer.

Companies of the age – which were a far cry from what one understands as corporations or companies now, as they were vehicles of colonization and self-government and not economic actors – were also at the forefront of political acts and reforms. In 1619, the Virginia Company effectively introduced representative democracy in the American colonies through its General Assembly, which elected the superior bureaucrats in the company. A few years later, the Massachusets Company did the same. By the late 1870s, the Senate was overun by the influence of companies – there were senators of various industries and they could be identified with ease, much more so than today, prompting president Rutherford B. Hayes to decry the situation: "all laws on corporations, on taxation, on trusts, wills, descent, and the like, need examination and extensive change. This is a government of the people, by the people, and for the people no longer. It is a government of corporations, by corporations, and for corporations."[3] Companies all around the world – acting on their own profit-making interest by now – started to alter the way in which people lived. They built skyscrapers and actual villages from scratch,

---

[1] John Micklethwait and Adrian Wooldridg, "Imperialists and speculators, 1500-1750," in *The Company: A Short History of A Revolutionary Idea* (New York and Toronto: Random House Canada, 2003).

[2] John Micklethwait and Adrian Wooldridge, *The Company: A Short History of A Revolutionary Idea* (New York and Toronto: Random House Canada, 2003).

[3] Charles Richard Williams, *Diary and Letters of Rutherford Birchard Hayes: Nineteenth President of the United States* (Ulan Press, 2012).

developing regions that had been smoldering in the ashes of war and poverty for hundreds of years. The age of the company had begun and soon enough it was in full swing.

Companies, however, do die, but in their own way. The East India Trading Company, for example, once a giant of wealth and power, lost its monopoly in 1813, was faced with the Indian Mutiny of 1857 and in 1873 it finally ceased to exist after a history of 273 years,[4] brought down by shifting new socio-political circumstances and fiercer competition. A product of its age, the HEIC could not thrive in an entirely different context than the one which required its existence in the first place.

After the two World Wars and the economic shifts they brought about, the nature of the company changed together with society, following different models of organization. Family-run companies were sold off or taken over by entire boards of investors; states chose "national champions" that competed on the international stage and finally Silicon Valley up-ended an entire economic model based on production capacity and the scale economies, replacing it with creativity and innovation. By the 1980s, the Soviet Union could produce thousands of tractors each week in its overgrown factories – but a garage in California could invent the future.

Micklethwait and Wooldridge conclude the origins story of the company by stating that "what often began as a state-sponsored charity has sprawled into all sorts of fields, reconfiguring geography, warfare, the arts, science, and sadly, the language. Companies have proved enormously powerful not just because they improve productivity, but also because they possess most of the legal rights of a human being, without the attendant disadvantages of biology: they are not condemned to die of old age and they create progeny pretty much at will."[5]

And yet the untapped political and social power and potential of the corporation was not immediately obvious – not with the advent of the internet and the interconnectivity it brought and not even with the fast-paced globalization facilitated by a newfound faith in free trade from the part of the governments of the world. Corporations were money-making machines, service providers and manufacturers of goods. Naturally, they had interests that could have been serviced to a larger extent by a politician, party or government rather than another but it was for the society of individual citizens to judge,

---

[4] "East India Company," Encyclopedia Britannica, accessed March 14th 2019, https://www.britannica.com/topic/East-India-Company.
[5] Micklethwait and Wooldridge, *The Company*, 15.

vote and voice their opinions, just as it had been for kings, queens and emperors to create and undo the companies of old.

Soon enough, however, corporations would find their own voice as well. That would only happen with *Citizens United.*

Chapter II

The Ruling

The *Citizens United* ruling of 2010 given by the United States Supreme Court held that political spending is a form of speech protected under the First Amendment and that the identity of the speaker is of no importance, and that it is speech itself that is protected, not the person who does the speaking. As a result, the United States government, the Court ruled, cannot keep corporations or unions from spending money in support or against individual candidates in elections, for that would be censoring speech. At the same time, while they cannot give money directly to campaigns, corporations may buy ads in support or against a candidate, per their right to free speech.

In order to understand the intentions behind the *Citizens United* ruling, one must look to its makers. Dubbed by many as the author of the ruling, United States Justice Anthony Kennedy delivered the majority opinion of the court on January 21st, 2010. In the first paragraph, it is clear that the Court issues a revision and overruling of the previous cases of *Austin*[1] and *McConnell*,[2] which placed limits on electioneering communication by corporations and unions. "Government may regulate corporate political speech through disclaimer and disclosure requirements, but it may not suppress that speech altogether,"[3] stated Kennedy before turning to the case in hand, namely the right of the nonprofit corporation *Citizens United* to release a critical film regarding then-candidate for the 2008 presidential primary elections Hillary Clinton. Corporations were about to receive – or rather, have enshrined – the right to free speech, but the disclaimer and disclosure requirements made it obligatory for them to reveal themselves through transparent contributions as *the* speaker whenever one corporation chose to finance a campaign.

Federal law prohibits corporations from using their money for electioneering communication, defined by the Court as "any broadcast, cable, or satellite communication" that "refers to a clearly identified candidate for Federal office" made before a general or primary election. The Court disagrees with the nonprofit *Citizens United* that the film it intended to air merely presented

---

[1] Austin v. Michigan Chamber of Commerce, 494 U. S. 652 (1990).
[2] McConnell v. Federal Election Committee, 540 U. S. 93, 203–209 (2003).
[3] Citizens United v. Federal Election Commission, 558 U.S. 310 (2010).

"historical events," holding that "the there is no reasonable interpretation of *Hillary* [the film] other than as an appeal to vote against Senator Clinton.[4] Seeking to distribute the movie it had made regarding Hillary Clinton on demand to prospective viewers, *Citizens United* argued that the restrictions placed on its "electioneering communication" were an unconstitutional ban on free speech, regardless of the intent of the ad itself.

Through Kennedy's voice, the Supreme Court reminded that "the First Amendment provides that 'Congress shall make no law ... abridging the freedom of speech'" and that such "laws enacted to control or suppress speech may operate at different points in the speech process." A ban on free speech was a ban no matter where it was imposed during the process of speaking, Kennedy made clear. According to the opinion of the Court, therefore, section 441b pertaining to "contributions or expenditures by national banks, corporations, or labor organizations" of the United States Code of Bills and Statues of 2006, "is an outright ban [on freedom of speech], backed by criminal sanctions"[5] and "is a ban on corporate speech notwithstanding the fact that a PAC created by a corporation can still speak."[6] According to the Court, the PAC exemption from section 441b does not mean that corporations are allowed to speak, not to mention that PACs have regulations to comply with themselves, which "might explain why fewer than 2,000 of the millions of corporations in the country have PACs."[7] Corporations have no free speech, even if they can establish Political Action Committees, or PACs – and so few of them do.

Citing *Buckley*,[8] Kennedy finally argued that "political speech must prevail against laws that would suppress it, whether by design or inadvertence."[9] Turning to the 2000 case of *United States v. Playboy Entertainment Group*[10] – a case in which the Playboy Group had claimed that Telecommunications Act of 1996, which required cable television operators managing adult programs to scramble or block those channels until hours during which children were unlikely to watch television, was violating the First Amendment and won, according to a Court opinion read by the same Kennedy –, the Justice showed that content-based restriction of speech is illegal. Kennedy also argued against restrictions on free speech that distinguishes between speakers, as "speech restriction based on the identity of the speaker is all too often simply a means

---

[4] Citizens United v. Federal Election Commission, 558 U.S. 310 (2010).
[5] Citizens United v. Federal Election Commission, 558 U.S. 310 (2010).
[6] Citizens United v. Federal Election Commission, 558 U.S. 310 (2010).
[7] Citizens United v. Federal Election Commission, 558 U.S. 310 (2010).
[8] Buckley v. Valeo, 424 U.S. 1 (1976).
[9] Buckley v. Valeo, 424 U.S. 1 (1976).
[10] United States v. Playboy Entertainment Group, Inc., 529 U. S. 803, 813 (2000).

to control the content."[11] Content and identity-based restrictions on speech were both infringing on the First Amendment. The only cases in which the Court upholds restrictions placed on speech is when they interfere with "the capacity of the government to discharge its [military] responsibilities," as made clear by the 1974 *Parker v. Levy* case.[12]

Finally, citing a plethora of cases such as the 1936 case of *Grosjean v. American Press*, which stipulates that political speech does not lose First Amendment protection "simply because its source is a corporation,"[13] or the 1978 case of *First National Bank of Boston v. Belloti,*[14] according to which states cannot regulate donations from corporations in ballot initiative campaigns, Kennedy concluded that "the Court has recognized that First Amendment protection extends to corporations."[15] Hinted at or partly conferred before, the United States Supreme Court now recognized corporations as being able to *speak* – and as a result having their speech protected.

Following Kennedy's momentous role in Citizens United and other cases, his announcement of retirement from the United States Supreme Court in July 2018 marked the start of a bitter debate over his legacy. Praised by liberals for his socially progressive decisions, Kennedy nevertheless "transformed the case [*Citizens United*] from a technical ruling on election regulation to a blockbuster that upended a century of law."[16] His impact on the *Citizens United v. FEC* case is reckoned by critics to have given the wealthiest Americans an upper hand in politics through campaign financing.[17] Moreover, Kennedy was accused of having no political experience and thus, no concept of what the consequences of his ruling would be.

A look into the background of this important backer of the *Citizens United* ruling may prove instructive. Kennedy was nominated to the Supreme Court by Republican president Ronald Reagan in 1988 and was often a swing vote in monumental decisions. His passion for individual rights and limited government is thus easier to understand, as the former Republican president is

---

[11] Citizens United v. Federal Election Commission, 558 U.S. 310 (2010).

[12] Parker v. Levy, 417 U. S. 733, 759 (1974).

[13] Grosjean v. American Press Co., 297 U. S. 233, 244 (1936).

[14] First Nat. Bank of Boston v. Bellotti, 435 U. S. 765, 778 (1978).

[15] Citizens United v. Federal Election Commission, 558 U.S. 310 (2010).

[16] "Did US Justice Anthony Kennedy Just Destroy His Own Legacy?" *Politico*, July 28th, 2018, https://www.politico.eu/article/did-us-supreme-court-justice-anthony-kennedy-just-destroy-his-own-legacy/.

[17] Ian Millhiser, "Justice Kennedy deserves this nasty, unflinching sendoff," *Think Progress*, June 27th, 2018, https://thinkprogress.org/kennedy-was-a-bad-justice-76e4640 24d78/.

commonly held as a champion of both. In guarding individual rights, however, Kennedy sided with protecting gay rights, in *Obergefell v. Hodges* and other cases, but also religious exercise, in the case of *Masterpiece Cakeshop*. He extended *habeas corpus* protections to detainees of the prison which is famously outside the reach of US-made laws, Guantanamo Bay, but also granted corporations the right of free speech, through *Citizens United* and *Buckley v. Valeo*, prompting lower courts to allow SuperPACs to gain a newfound power in the political sphere.

Often invoked in debates surrounding *Citizens United* or free speech, the *Buckley* case proved to be a stepping stone. *Buckley* signaled that while money is not speech in itself, it facilitates and incentivizes it, acting as a support, and therefore, placing restrictions on giving and spending money means, in effect, limiting speech. While money is not speech per se, the latter could not manifest itself without the former and thus, for all intents and purposes, they are the same.

The same line of thinking can be applied to numerous other constitutionally-protected rights, according to Hellman. She stresses that the connection between money and speech does not mean that limiting the former impacts the latter, just like "one has the right to private sexual intimacy, but not to spend money to facilitate the exercise of that right"[18] – although, in practice, history has shown otherwise. What is missing is a general theory about rights and money, one that *Buckley* did not provide, and one that will be sketched in the following paragraphs.

In almost any scenario, money empowers an individual – but also an entity like a corporation. A relationship between two actors cannot be equal if one has excessive amounts of money and the other none at all. If one is to connect money to speech, critics of *Citizens United* hold, it means recognizing that some people have *stronger* rights than others, thus infringing on the foundational promises of liberal democracy. Moreover, if giving money always carries the constitutional right of free speech, then all economic activities could be judged through the lens of rights.

But nuance is important here. In the 1977 case of *Abood v. Detroit Board of Education*, the Supreme Court held that non-union public employees had to pay a share in the "agency shop" allowed by the Michigan law at the time even if they did not support it – but their money could not be used for activities that they did not endorse, such as political contributions. What happened in reality, however, was that the fees paid by non-members freed up other amounts of

---

[18] Deborah Hellman, "Money Talks but it isn't Speech," *Minnesota Law Review* 102, 6 (2011): pp. 952-1002.

money that could be used for spending on political campaigns,[19] thus arriving at the same outcome that was intended to be avoided, namely the rise of union spending on political campaigns. At the same time, giving money was considered, in the context of the *Abood* case and in the reasoning of the Justices, as less important than spending it – it is there that speech came into play, in the same way as taxes are not speech, but campaign contributions are. In 2018, *Abood* was overruled in a 5-to-4 decision in *Janus v. AFCME*, the Justices of the Roberts court describing the 1977 precedent as "poorly reasoned."[20] Instead, the Court rejected the obligation of non-members of unions of public enterprises to pay membership fees, which, as shown before, freed up other amounts of money that were used in ways to which non-members of unions did not assent. Taxes may not be speech, but they may – despite the opposition of the taxpayer – still lead to the buying of bombs or the financing of state propaganda.

According to Hellman, the relationship between money and speech has three parts – money can provide incentives to speak, it can facilitate speaking and finally giving and spending money can themselves be expressive. Following her, only the last part is connected to the First Amendment.[21] Moreover, the intent accompanying the act of giving must also be understood by those who view the act or receive the money. When one is buying an apple, it should not, therefore, be considered speech. When one makes a contribution to an agrarian party that vowed to only support apple-pickers, for example, then money equals speech.

But the politically-conscious corporations and their recognized ability of free speech, manifested through campaign contributions, fit all three of Hellman's described parts of the relationship between money and speech. Firstly, corporations are incentivized to speak (i.e. contribute to campaigns or take public stances on social and political issues through ads and statements) by their existential need to obtain profit. This happens because certain political speech is conducive to the retaining and the acquiring of new consumers – who respond to such speech monetarily, by buying the corporation's products in order to show support, as happened with Nike in the aftermath of the Colin

---

[19] Megan McArdle, "Why you should care about the Supreme Court's Janus decision," *The Washington Post*, June 27th, 2018, https://www.washingtonpost.com/opinions/the-su preme-court-may-have-killed-collective-bargaining/2018/06/27/9b19bbc6-7a3c-11e 8-aeee-4d04c8ac6158_story.html.
[20] Justice Alito cited in McArdle, "Why you should care about the Supreme Court's Janus decision," https://www.washingtonpost.com/opinions/the-supreme-court-may-have-killed-collective-bargaining/2018/06/27/9b19bbc6-7a3c-11e8-aeee-4d04c8ac6158_sto ry.html.
[21] Hellman, "Money Talks but it isn't Speech," 952-1002.

Kaepernick ads – and thus maximizing profit. Secondly, money spent by corporations obviously facilitates speaking, as corporations speak through financing ads or campaigns and ensuring visibility. In the absence of money, such as in the case of a small-to-medium size company, speech is also absent. Thirdly, corporations spend their money in a way that is expressive in and of itself, by financing the political campaigns of candidates and parties that are progressive rather than conservative. For other corporations, the reverse is true, as they cater to conservative categories of consumers whom, like the progressives, also require representation from *their* corporations.

Returning to the *Buckley* case, in which the Court argued that speech – or more exactly, "some forms of communication"[22] – is made possible by money, but that sometimes money and conduct reunite to produce speech, one can see a recognition of the complex nature of speech – and how such a definition of speech can be used to grant corporations First Amendment protections.

In the body of the 2010 *Citizens United* decision, the opinions of the composing Justices of the United States Supreme Court reveal the divisions, debates and interpretations that circulated among them before the ruling. Justice Stevens, a Republican up until his nomination in 1975 – and who subsequently retired in the same year as the *Citizens United* ruling – was the most ardent opponent of the ruling in *Citizens United*, and he pleaded his case as a Justice, within the Court, and even after his retirement before Congress. After expressing his dissatisfaction regarding the way in which the Supreme Court was broadening the initially narrow scope of the case and was now expressly ruling against the precedent cases of *Austin* and *McConnell*, Stevens expressed the minority opinion and argued that "corporations have no consciences, no beliefs, no feelings, no thoughts, no desires." Corporations, according to Stevens, are structures that facilitate human activity and whose personhood is limited to the concept of "useful legal fictions," and cannot be considered part of the well-known formulation of the Constitution "We the People."[23]

Stevens went on, making explicit his embrace of a limited form of the "amalgamation" theory in stating that it is individuals who exercise their free speech rights, while business corporations cannot even be thought of as facilitating these rights. The Framers of the United States Constitution, Steven says, could not have imagined that corporate speakers would be placed on par with individuals, much less that such an interpretation "would preclude legislatures from taking limited measures to guard against corporate capture of

---

[22] Buckley v. Valeo, 424 U.S. 1 (1976).
[23] Citizens United v. Federal Election Committee, 558 U.S. (2010), p. 76.

elections."[24] Instead, Stevens argued that Congress and state legislatures should be allowed to impose "reasonable limits" to the amount of money that a candidate or his backers may spend during a campaign.[25] The vagueness of what constitutes "reasonable" was perhaps one of the most important reasons for which Stevens and likeminded Justices remained the minority in the *Citizens United* case, his solution being rejected by the majority of the Supreme Court Justices.

In commenting the case, Tribe labels Stevens' solution as just another case of the "'I know it when I see it' ad-hockery that plagued the Court's midcentury attempts to define obscenity."[26] In *Austin*, the Court, through the voice of Justice Marshall, had defended the Michigan Campaign Finance Act, which banned corporations from making expenditures in elections – even through PACs – by citing the uneven influence that they may have on the process,[27] especially when compared to the expenses made toward the same goal by a single individual. However, just as in Stevens' opinion in *Citizens United*, that left the interpretation of "unfair" to the political legislative majorities, which used the vague ruling in partisan way so as to limit the resources of the opposition. *Austin* was flawed, and its faults worsened the political struggle at the state legislative level until it was overruled by *Citizens United*.

In the *Citizens United* case, Justice Scalia, with whose opinion Justices Alito and Thomas concurred, offered another interpretation. In his view, the First Amendment cannot be taken to exclude the freedom of the press, meaning the "conduct of artificial legal entities."[28] Even at the time of the Framers, Scalia says, journalists expressed their freedom of speech through newspapers, "which (much like corporations) had their own names, outlived the individuals who had founded them, could be bought and sold, were sometimes owned by more than one person, and were operated for profit."[29] In this way, Scalia and his supporters can be viewed as adopting the "real entity" model – newspapers, being corporations, always had a life of their own, outside the reach of their founders, editors or journalists, and were thus always included in the protections awarded by the First Amendment.

At the same time, Scalia partly concurred with the majority and maintained that "the [First] Amendment is written in terms of 'speech,' not speakers. Its text

---

[24] Citizens United v. Federal Election Committee, 558 U.S. (2010), pp. 36-37.

[25] Laurence H. Tribe, "Dividing 'Citizens United': The Case v. The Controversy," *Constitutional Commentary* 30, 2 (Summer 2015): pp. 463-494.

[26] Tribe, "Dividing 'Citizens United'," 469.

[27] Austin v. Michigan Chamber of Commerce, 494 U. S. 652 (1990).

[28] Citizens United v. Federal Election Committee, 558 U.S. (2010), pp. 6-7.

[29] Citizens United v. Federal Election Committee, 558 U.S. (2010).

offers no foothold for excluding any category of speakers, from single individuals to partnerships of individuals, to unincorporated associations of individuals, to incorporated associations of individuals [...], to exclude or impede corporate speech is to muzzle the principal agents of the modern free economy. We should celebrate rather than condemn the addition of this speech to the public debate."[30]

The flaws and misinterpretations of the Justices in the case were highlighted by critics from the left and the right. According to Tribe the broad nature of the Court's interpretation in *Citizens United* – a recurring flaw in the Court headed by Chief Justice Roberts – went much beyond the initial question posed by the parties in the case itself, representing an overreach by the Supreme Court. In broadening the scope of the question, the Court also adopted the "narrowest possible view of corruption, maintaining that the only legitimate government interest in this field is the prevention of *quid pro quo* corruption."[31] Naïve to the kind of backstage dealings that populate the political sphere of the United States, the Justices meant to revitalize the concept of free speech but may have, instead, ensured a lasting bond between corporations and politicians. As the present book argues, however, such a bond predated *Citizens United* – and it is by now antiquated, as corporations are *becoming politicians* themselves, as chapter IX will show.

The majority of USSC Justices defended their opinion regarding the *Citizens United* case by stating that while it is most definitely true that the Framers wrote the First Amendment with individual men and women in mind, "the individual person's right to speak includes the right to speak *in association with other individual persons.*"[32] Kennedy's forceful defense of the ruling could be traced back to his dissenting opinion in *Austin*, where he stated that "all speakers, including individuals and the media, use money amassed from the economic marketplace to fund their speech. The First Amendment protects the resulting speech, even if it was enabled by economic transactions with persons or entities who disagree with the speaker's ideas."[33] Moreover, the entire *Citizens United v. FEC* case is predicated, according to the majority, not on the character of the film promoted by Citizens United of being "speech", but on the identity of the speaker – in this case, a corporation. The minority opinion and other critics of the decision may attempt to silence speech by questioning the

---

[30] Citizens United v. Federal Election Committee, 558 U.S. (2010).
[31] Tribe, "Dividing 'Citizens United'," 483.
[32] Citizens United v. Federal Election Committee, 558 U.S. (2010).
[33] Austin v. Michigan Chamber of Commerce, 494 U.S. 652, 707 (1990) as cited in Tribe, "Dividing 'Citizens United,'" 469.

identity of the speaker – and according to the majority of Justice in the United States Supreme Court, such an advent infringes on the First Amendment.

Citizens United was not even the final step in the extension of rights to corporations. Drawing on the first corporate case right, that of *Bank of the United States* v. *Deveaux*, in 1809, to the *Hobby Lobby* case of 2014, Adam Winkler highlights the path that corporations took in winning their rights, in spite of being left out of the foundational documents of the United States. Corporations won more and more rights as decades went by through the courts, and the *Citizens United* and *Hobby Lobby* cases are simply the culmination of that process. As "Ronald McDonald and the Pillsbury Doughboy never marched on Washington or protested down Main Street with signs demanding equal rights for corporations,"[34] the corporations rode the wave of favorable U.S. Supreme Court decisions in order to obtain their rights, often to the dismay of the public. Despite *Citizens United*, it was a revolutionizing concept of corporate personhood that drove the expansion of corporate rights. Winkler argues that the association or *amalgamation* model that appeared in the aftermath of *Santa Clara* still functions as the main line of thinking for the Supreme Court justices, as made clear by Justice Alito in the *Hobby Lobby* case. The Hobby Lobby stores could enjoy religious liberty because the Court viewed it as an extension of the religious liberty of the Green family, its owners. Even now, therefore, there is no official, legal recognition of corporations as entities imbued with a life of their own – and the free speech they now enjoy is a byproduct of the free speech of those individuals that make up the corporations. But that is only the current state of a century-old legal battle waged by corporations – and, as history demonstrates, the corporate overlords have nothing but patience.

One could say that in *Citizens United*, the Supreme Court, through the voice of Justice Kennedy, preferred to give a categorical protection to the freedom of speech, rather than get lost in the complexities of distinguishing between speakers for the sake of practical equality in electoral competitions. In good conservative fashion, the Court's 5 to 4 majority was more favorable to allowing corporations to have an unequally powerful voice in the political sphere rather than open the Pandora box of government-imposed limitations on political speech – based on speaker – and thus lay an enormous stress on the First Amendment.

To sum up, one can safely say that in 2010 the majority of United States Supreme Court Justices concluded that criticizing a presidential hopeful is core

---

[34] Adam Winkler, *We the Corporations: How American Businesses Won Their Civil Rights* (London and New York: W.W. Norton and Company, 2018), 12.

political speech and that its character as speech could not change even if the speaker was a corporation. Nevertheless, this line of argumentation from the majority of Justices prompts a discussion on judicial and political personhood. Despite the outcry that followed the decision, in *Citizens United* the Court did not innovate to a grand degree. Successive legal theories had been grasping at corporations for two centuries. As the following chapter will show, acknowledging the free speech of corporations was not a destination that the Supreme Court simply chanced upon, it was the end-result of an arduous battle that challenged fundamental legal and political notions.

Chapter III

Corporatist Theories

The previous chapter recounted the legal journey that the Supreme Court went on to arrive at its ruling in the *Citizens United* case. It showed that the highest judicial body in the United States took into consideration different interpretation and issues connected to campaign finance, free speech, and personhood before making its ruling. But *Citizens United* is not the first encounter corporations had with political rights throughout the years. Before obtaining free speech and thus the role of *speaker*, therefore personhood, companies had been subjected to three theories that sought to explain their existence and their role in society.

The earliest corporatist theory stated that corporations are creatures of the state, which created them and upon which their continued existence depends in a most intimate manner. This "artificial person" or "concession" theory, as it is called, evolved in the early 19th century and rested on the view that a corporation effectively exists at the sufferance of the state and, therefore, is not entitled to any rights or protections not granted to it by statute.[1] The corporation could not assert its rights against its benefactor, the state itself. At that time, companies were entrusted with monopolies by the state and as such, competition was non-existent. Those who worked for these early companies could have, in effect, been working for the state, save for the independent owners and managers – usually nobles – who profited greatly from their "businesses." In such a state of affairs, the corporation was indeed a subsidiary of the state, as it could not have survived without the government-ensured monopolies which were the subject of its activity. The forces currently at play within the contemporary globalized market, specifically the empowered consumer, had not yet formed. Each company of the age serviced a localized area, usually a sole country, which had its citizens starved for variety in terms of goods and services, the latter situation being prolonged by the monopoly system. In this market setting, the state created the company by allowing it access to the consumer – and for monopolies, this immediately became the opposite of the contemporary consumers' market, namely a *seller's market*, one in which the seller gets to set the terms of the process of buying and selling of

---

[1] Stefan Padfield, "Rehabilitating Concession Theory," *Oklahoma Law Review* 66, 2 (2013): pp. 327-361.

goods. Today, both practice and theory in corporate law marginalize the "concession."

The conceptual framework and the market realities put in place by the "concession" theory shifted with the *County of Santa Clara v. Southern Pacific Rail Co.*[2] case of 1886, which started when the Southern Pacific Railway Company refused to pay taxes on its fences at the higher rate stipulated by the state of California for companies. As a result of the case, the United States Supreme Court changed its interpretation of the existence of corporations from one of mere creatures of the state to one which stated that corporations held the status of personhood for purposes of the Fourteenth Amendment, meaning citizenship rights and equal protection of the laws[3] - but the unanimous opinion of the Justices never expressly stated this. Because of *Santa Clara*, however, the lower courts held that a corporation cannot be taxed differently than natural persons. Within this model, a corporation is seen as an amalgamation of the people who stand behind it. Thus, according to this "amalgamation" or "aggregate" model, it was appropriate to grant the corporation rights in order to protect the rights of the people behind it – and to not infringe on corporate rights in order to not infringe on the individual rights of the shareholders and owners of said corporation. The term "amalgamation" itself is usually attributed to the process of merging two or more companies and their assets and liabilities into a new entity – this time, however, the "amalgamated" were the individuals who formed the corporation, *merging their rights* into it. With this second definition, the story of the corporation was inching closer to the supercitizen-corporation of the present day. However, it was clear that the interpretation of the Justices in *Santa Clara* was that companies could not be divorced from their founders, owners, managers and even workers. There was no independent personhood or drives behind the company other than those of its owners.

Influenced by the then-innovative combination of politics and economy of Downs, Buchanan or Tullock, March[4] tried to propose a revised theory of the business firm in 1962, one which assigned the role of political coalition to the company and that of political broker to its executive. In this view, the corporation has no personhood of itself – it was to be considered a miniature polity, *a political conflict system* in which the CEOs bargain and negotiate with

---

[2] Santa Clara County v. Southern Pacific R. Co., 118 U.S. 394 (1886).

[3] Pierre-Yves Neron, "Rethinking the Ethics of Corporate Political Activities in Post-Citizens United Era: Political Equality, Corporate Citizenship and Market Failures," *Journal of Business Ethics* 136 (October 2015): pp. 5-35.

[4] James G. March, "The Business Firm as a Political Coalition." The Journal of Politics 24, 4 (November 1962): pp. 662-678 https://doi.org/10.2307/2128040.

those making demands – employees, stockholders – not unlike elected officials do within a given state apparatus and international context. Working under the intellectual currents of his time, the early 1960s, and the dominating political and economic theories of the time, together with their faults, March has the impressive merit of seeing how economy and politics merge together. However, while he envisioned a *politicization* of the economic, the trend ever since has been to *economize* politics, in practice and in theory – with calls from the part of the U.S. electorate for the country to be run like a business or simply have the "greatest businesspeople in the world"[5] run the country. March's theory, however, is still irrevocably tied to "natural" persons, individuals, and does not consider the fact that corporations themselves can be political actors.

At the turn of the twentieth century, a third model of corporation theory emerged among scholars: the "real entity" model. It rested on the premise that the corporation is an entity unto itself, separate and apart from the authorization of the state and any natural persons who might at any particular time control it. In continuation of the main defense of the "amalgamation" theory, namely that a corporation was constituted by its members – in the case of the company, its shareholders –, supporters of the "real entity" theory argued that once constituted, the corporation was a distinct *person* that could not be reduced to any number of its constituting members. The corporation was an avatar of the group of people behind it, and as such, it was more than its parts, it was an entity unto itself – as Canfield commented in 1917, "the contracts and torts of a corporation are its contracts and torts, and not those of its members."[6]

This interpretation of the company was expressly going against the two previous ones. In a sense, a *corporation became a person* — an entity with status and rights that should be recognized under the constitution and laws. The courts subsequently recognized that corporations may have First Amendment rights when it came to ballot initiatives through statements and endorsements. As such, a corporation could "speak" about a certain piece of legislation – because its individual, constituting members or shareholders could – but until *Citizens United*, its right to speech — i.e. its own direct spending on elections— was curtailed.[7] This suggests that the Court thought of corporations as political persons of a sort, as they pertained to the First Amendment, but only to the

---

[5] "Final Trump-Clinton Debate Transcript for the 2016 presidential elections," *The Washington Post*, October 20th, 2016, https://www.washingtonpost.com/news/the-fix/wp/2016/10/19/the-final-trump-clinton-debate-transcript-annotated.
[6] George Canfield, "The Scope and Limits of the Corporate Entity Theory," *Columbia Law Review* 17, 2 (February 1917): pp. 129.
[7] Michael Phillips, "Reappraising the Real Entity Theory of the Corporation," *Florida State University Law Review* 21, 4 (Spring 1994): pp. 1061-1123.

extent that their interests did not interfere with the interests of "natural" citizens in their democracy. The overlords were still awfully silent, but soon they were about to gain a voice that would surpass the regulation-laden murmur.

After *Citizens United*, it became clear that if campaign contributions were speech, the voice of corporations could not be ignored. The clash between the will of a company and that of an individual necessarily gave the former as a clear winner. As such, the study of campaign contributions became a natural recurrence in the American political and electoral scene – Rinner identifies a 1976 case as the starting point for modern campaign finance regulation and jurisprudence.[8]

In the 1976 case of *Buckley v. Valeo*, the Supreme Court partly overturned the Federal Election Campaign Act of 1971, finding expenditure limits unconstitutional but allowing limits to be imposed on contribution and public funding provisions.[9] Moreover, "the Court found that the $1000 limit on individual contributions was directly aligned with 'the Act's primary purpose— to limit the actuality and appearance of corruption resulting from large individual financial contributions,' which could amount to a "political *quid pro quo*."[10] In effect, the Court recognized that limiting expenditure was limiting speech, but maintained that contributions were different, and that capping them was paramount to the fight against the corruption that the corporate money bags would undoubtedly bring.

In *Buckley*, political stability took precedence over the political rights of the judicially-recognized "artificial persons" – corporations. As the years went on and as these cases were being judged, public opinion remained uninformed and indifferent. The legal mumbo-jumbo seemed without any connection to reality: what was the difference between expenditure and contributions and how would that sway political campaigns, altering, in turn, American democracy? After *Citizens United*, however, the individual woke before a deserted battlefield - and a battle that he had already and unknowingly lost. Once awake, however, he was scandalized, and began to criticize. With regard to *Citizens United*, critics abound and make use not only of the judicial approach, but the historical one as well. The next chapter details the arguments of Adam Winkler, one of the notable critics of the heritage of corporatist theories in general – and of *Citizens United* in particular. For Winkler, a simple

---

[8] William Rinner, "Maximizing Participation Through Campaign Finance Regulation: A Cap and Trade Mechanism for Political Money," *The Yale Law Journal* 119, 5 (March 2010): pp. 1060-1121.

[9] Buckley v. Valeo, 424 U.S. 1 (1976).

[10] Federal Election Campaign Act of 1971, Pub. L. No. 92-225, 86 Stat. 3 (1972) as quoted in Rinner, "Maximizing Participation," 5.

clerical error allowed corporations to hijack the Fourteenth Amendment, designed for freed slaves, and shelter themselves from regulation under the pretense that they are persons.

Chapter IV

The Drafting of a False History

The outcome of the *Citizens United* case, as detailed in the previous chapter, became the latest theory framing corporations as *persons* endowed with rights. According to this theory, the separate entity that is the corporation not only aggregates the interests and rights of its constituting members but has rights of its own that are in turn divorced from those of the members. This has been criticized in a number of ways. While the mainstream form of criticism says that viewing corporations as "artificial persons" with rights such as freedom of speech is just an excuse for high-level executives and the rich to gleefully spend their money on political campaigns and thus decisively influence elections,[1] a more specialized criticism aims at the heart of the latest theory of corporate personhood by challenging its legal history. According to Adam Winkler,[2] the whole spectacle surrounding the *Citizens United* ruling actually originated more than a century ago, in the 1880s, when a lawyer representing one of the largest corporations of the day lied to the Supreme Court. To prove his case, Winkler goes back to the *Santa Clara* case but looks neither at the Court's ruling nor at the opinions of the Justices, but at the lawyer that the *Southern Pacific Railroad* company employed.

The lawyer was Roscoe Conkling, himself twice nominated to the Supreme Court, but who refused both times despite his confirmation by the Senate, and the corporation was the by-now-familiar Southern Pacific Railroad Company. At that time, railroads were the most advanced, largest and most independent companies in existence. Their activity ran across multiple states and required the employment of tens of thousands, and Southern Pacific was one of the largest railroad companies in the United States.

In order to defend the railroad company against a special tax instituted by California, Conkling invoked the Fourteenth Amendment, originally meant to protect the rights of freed slaves after the Civil War. According to Conkling, every "person" had to have equal protection of the laws. The lawyer then argued that the company was a *person* like any other and that it should enjoy the same

---

[1] Bertrall L. Ross II, "Addressing Inequality in the Age of Citizens United," *New York University Law Review* 93, 5 (2018): pp. 1132-1135.
[2] Winkler, *We the Corporations*, 10.

treatment as any other individual. He had every right to the interpretation, seeing as in the 1860s, then-congressman Conkling was part of the drafting committee[3] which wrote the same Amendment, and was the only living member of that committee during the Southern Pacific Railroad hearing. Speaking with the authority of memory, Conkling stated that the original intention of the drafting committee was to include corporations into the category of "persons," which replaced that of "citizens."

So far so good, says Winkler, only that later on it was proven that such an intention never existed.[4]

Nevertheless, suspicious of Conkling's claims even then, the Supreme Court debated the case for three years. Eventually, the matter was finally settled by the corporation through an understanding and the political and constitutional system remained unchanged. Years later, however, a case presenting the exact same question was brought to the same Court by the same company – the case which will become the *Santa Clara* case discussed in the previous chapter –, this time without the legal representation of Conkling. In this second case, the Supreme Court abandoned the "concession" theory, held the "amalgamation" theory as being true and refused to acknowledge corporations as persons – only as unions of persons. The result is well-known by now – companies could not be taxed differently than individuals because this would infringe on the individual rights of their constituting members, shareholders or owners. And yet, they were not persons.

One judge, however, disagreed with his peers. His name was Stephen J. Field, and he was rumored to have shared internal memoranda of the Justices with Southern Pacific's legal team. In the minority, Field had his hands tied until the clerk in charge of editing the volumes containing the official opinions of the Supreme Court judges, officially called the "reporter of decisions," made a mistake. By the name of J.C. Bancroft Davis, the clerk registered that the Court had ruled that "corporations are persons within the Fourteenth Amendment," even though in general they should be regarded as unions of persons.[5] Years later, armed with Davis' mistake in record, the rebelling Field started to refer to the *Santa Clara County v. Southern Pacific Railroad* case, in which the Court had unquestionably ruled that corporations are persons. His strategy worked,

---

[3] Winkler, *We the Corporations*, 132.

[4] Adam Winkler, "'Corporations Are People' is built on an incredible 19th-century lie," *The Atlantic*, March 5th, 2018, https://www.theatlantic.com/business/archive/2018/03/corporations-people-adam-winkler/554852/.

[5] Winkler, "'Corporations Are People' is built on an incredible 19th-century lie," https://www.theatlantic.com/business/archive/2018/03/corporations-people-adam-winkler/554852/.

and more citations following the same line appeared - amounting to 312 cases on the rights of corporations, compared to 28 involving the rights of African Americans, the original beneficiaries of the Fourteenth Amendment. And so, according to Winkler, an Amendment intended to protect minorities actually ended up, through the acts of Conkling, Field and Davis, only furthering the path of corporations to personhood and the rights and protections that flow from that status.

However, Winkler concedes that as corporations became liable for crimes around the early 1900s, they were eligible to enjoy the same protections given to criminal defendants by the Constitution, such as due process, reasonable doubt and property rights. These protections, however, do not amount to political freedom and religious conscience. Moreover, even in the *Citizens United* decision, Winkler highlights, the phrase "corporate personhood" is missing.[6] Just as absent is the word "corporation" in the United States Constitution, meaning that the foundational document of the country issues no protections to corporations. The *Federalist Papers*, as well, make no mention of corporations.

It is of no less importance to remember that in the days of the Founding Fathers, corporations themselves, in organizational forms recognizable to the contemporary mind, were nowhere to be seen.[7] And yet, by 2014, the Supreme Court had given corporations free speech – through *Citizens United* – and religious liberty – through the *Hobby Lobby* case, in which the Hobby Lobby craft stores chain was allowed to remove birth control from their employees' health plans due to the fact that the owners, the Green family, wanted to run its stores according to Biblical precepts.[8] Today, corporations enjoy not only free speech but also the right to worship.

As for the corporations, they had every motivation to seek constitutional rights and protections which would allow them to obtain more autonomy and a guarantee against the interference of state authorities with their ultimate goal – that of amassing profits. According to Winkler, the profit motive allowed corporations to influence policymaking and in courts of law throughout the history of the United States. Constitutional litigation was used by businesses against the public successfully time and time again, allowing corporate rights to expand and profits to soar. For corporations, litigation and lobbying – even using their armies of top lawyers simply as a deterrent against opposing

---

[6] "How American Corporations Had a 'Hidden' Civil Rights Movement," *NPR*, March 26th, 2018, https://www.npr.org/2018/03/26/596989664/how-american-corporations-had-a-hidden-civil-rights-movement.
[7] Winkler, *We the Corporations*, 155.
[8] Burwell v. Hobby Lobby Stores, Inc., 573 U.S. (2014).

lawmakers – was simply a cost-effective way to protect their financial gains, a mere cost of doing business. Whereas African-Americans and sexual minorities faced violence and suffering on an everyday basis in their fight for recognition and equality, oil companies and other industry giants pressured elected representatives and judges in order to increase their profits.

By exploiting legal reforms originally meant to help minorities and by innovating the system through constitutional litigation and precedent, corporations managed to win rights and protections and disentangle themselves from regulation. As such, the late-twentieth-century libertarian thought embodied by politicians such as Margaret Thatcher and Ronald Reagan was not the only driver of deregulation.

But the story involving corporations and the battle for rights does not stop there. It would be all too easy to condemn the for-profit companies for ruining American democracy as it was envisioned by the Founders. In fact, the litigation battles carried out by companies in their campaign for increased protections from the long arm of the American political system had some extraordinary by-products. Armed with the best lawyers and boundless resources, companies, Winkler admits, pioneered the first cases in which the Supreme Court struck down laws for violating the First Amendment and which later became the foundation for much more famous cases like *Brown* v. *Board of Education* and *Roe* v. *Wade*.[9]

In pursuing profit, corporations have often been the "unsung heroes of civil rights."[10] This, however, does not mean that their fight for protections does not merit close scrutiny or that it is entirely worthy of praise. As many other prolonged processes that involve politics, economy and law, the story of corporations and their legal battle for rights has its angels and demons – and no actor is clearly one or the other.

The next chapter abandons the legal sphere for the political and conceptual one, showing that corporations achieving recognition in the former also meant their integration into the latter. Clerical errors at a certain point or no, the Court, in over two centuries of debates and rulings, has created a new category of persons – even though their legal recognition is only the formalization of an already existing environment where corporations have had to become political actors to be economically successful. Now as self-standing, political persons, not creatures of the state, purely economic agents or unions of persons, corporations have to be acknowledged as constitutive parts of the society. The usual route for a person to achieve such a status goes through citizenship.

---

[9] Winkler, *We the Corporations*, 326.
[10] Winker, *We the Corporations*, 18.

Chapter V

Citizenship and the Corporation

The previous chapter recounted a powerful criticism against corporate personhood, one which argues that corporations have obtained rights and protections so far held only by individual, "natural" persons due to misinterpretations of the law and ill-intent. This line of criticism, however, completely disregards the representation duties ascribed nowadays to corporations by people, by consumers, which will be showcased in chapter IX. To use legal history to deny an unfolding reality simply amounts to covering one's eyes and ears and pretending that something is not really there, that corporations and companies are still purely economic agents concerned only with buying low and selling high. That Davis made a clerical error or that Field used that error to suit his ends does not mean that consumers today, according to their own beliefs, do or do not want to buy from companies that support same-sex marriage, source transparently or produce their goods in a facility detaining Uighurs. The political dimension of corporations does not escape all contemporary authors, even though almost all use an approach that is entirely different from the one of the present book. A recently popular way of integrating corporations into the societal, and therefore political, realm is to bestow citizenship upon them, to treat them as natural citizens through the same prism of citizenship.

In deciphering the meaning and implications of corporate citizenship with the tools provided by the history of political philosophy, Jeurissen[1] highlights four key parts of the concept of citizenship: the social contract, collective responsibility, active responsibility and the juridical state. Like individual citizens, the corporate citizen must present a moral commitment to adhere to the social contract, binding itself to it like the "natural" citizen subjects himself to the laws of the polity. Citizenship, according to Jeurissen, also implies an active participation in the community and a constant interest in the life of the *polis*. In this view, however, corporations, unlike "natural persons" are created – they do not exist in the natural state and must be made, thus requiring justification for their existence. That justification, of course, can be found in the social benefits that a corporation brings to the table. Corporate citizenship,

[1] Ronald Jeurissen, "Institutional conditions of corporate citizenship," *Journal of Business Ethics* 53 (August 2004): pp. 87-96.

then "is institutionally determined by how the external environment of the company sets the conditions for its socially responsible and sustainable policies."[2] When the legal environment of a polity discourages corporate citizenship, when stakeholders are passive and disinterested and when the cultural environment is discouraging towards corporate participation in the social life of the community, then corporations cannot possibly act as citizens.

However, Jeurissen also states that when the market presents a high degree of competition, then the room for corporate citizenship is reduced. By contrast, the present book argues that such a moment is precisely the time when corporations become active on the social and political spheres, with the express and profit-seeking goal of differentiating themselves and their products from the interchangeable products – perfect substitutes – of the competition, thus granting themselves a competitive edge on the fiercely competitive market.[3]

A momentous contribution to the present book is the work of Pierre-Yves Neron[4] and his investigation into the politically-active corporations. In a 2010 article tackling the subject, Neron presents an overview of the literature that involved corporations in politics. The theories he discusses present corporations as: a) distributive agents; b) political communities of themselves; c) as citizens or citizen-like entities; d) as active political actors. According to the first view, corporations are social institutions with societal impact. The second theory holds them as miniature political communities analogous to the state. In the third case, corporations and firms are the targets of traditionally left-leaning activists that are now pushing concepts such as "sustainable development" and "corporate social responsibility," rewarding the virtuous corporations and punishing those who transgress against the stated values. Finally, in the fourth and final case, corporations are actors that can "influence the construction of public policies, regulations, and laws" through "zealous lobbying, contributions to political action committees (PAC), public declarations, participation in public debates, provision of information, participation in public consultation processes, and so on."[5] This last direction, Neron notes, has been ignored in the specialized literature, which paints such actions taken by corporations as mere profit-seeking lobbying. The corporations themselves are not keen on shedding light onto their campaign

---

[2] Jeurissen, "Institutional conditions of corporate citizenship," 91.
[3] Water Nicholson and Christopher Snyder, *Microeconomic Theory: Basic Principles and Extensions* (Mason: Thomson South-Western, 2008), pp. 100-102
[4] Pierre-Yves Neron, "Business and the Polis: What Does it Mean to See Corporations as Political Actors?" *Journal of Business Ethics* 94, 3 (November 2009): pp. 333-352.
[5] Neron, "Business and the Polis," 343.

contributions or politician connections – taking environmental protection into account, Neron highlights that corporations "have fewer incentives to be transparent about how they lobbied to defeat stronger environmental regulations inspired by the protocol of Kyoto."[6] Indeed, such actions taken by corporations will go unnoticed, unpunished and unpoliticized if they are not seen by consumers or if they remain silent – in a monetary, *Citizens United*, groceries-as-votes sense – regarding the subject.

Writing five years before the *Citizens United* ruling of the United States Supreme Court, Moon, Crane and Matten ask in their eponymous article – can corporations be citizens? The answer they come up with is that even if incorporation "creates legal corporate identities with attendant rights and responsibilities" [...] "corporations nowhere are classified in terms of human citizenship."[7] At the same time, corporations can act "*in citizenly fashion*"[8] and that the private interests that they may carry to the public fore – such as ExxonMobil's interest in continuing the use of fossil fuels – is not unlike the interest of a private individual engaging in the same area. One would logically argue, however, that the two examples differ in capacities – Exxon can sway senators and representatives through the promise or the threat of withholding campaign contributions, whereas the individual, even when attempting to actively influence an elected official representing the state, may find his voice drowned in a sea of individuals attempting to do the same. The voice of Exxon booms throughout the halls of the US Congress, whereas that of the individual person is a whisper that merely makes it to the front door.

But what happens when society, through the voice of its consumers and their wallets, overwhelmingly points to a certain direction? The authors conclude that "the typical result, as seen in the cases of BP and Shell, is processes of self-regulation, which allow corporations to pursue societal demands in a fashion that is still compatible with their own corporate interests and goals."[9] In other words, acting under the public magnifying glass, corporations find a way to balance consumer wishes and their own interests, not unlike an elected official balances the wishes of his constituents and his own electoral goals. In this way, corporations can be incentivized, with the old carrot-or-stick approach, by the consumers to pursue a common good and not avoid spilling petrol into the ocean, burning down forests or poisoning streams.

---

[6] Neron, "Business and the Polis," 348.
[7] Jeremy Moon, Andrew Crane and Dirk Matten, "Can corporations be citizens? Corporate citizenship as a metaphor for business participation in society," *Business Ethics Quarterly* 15, 3 (July 2005): pp. 437 https://doi.org/10.5840/beq200515329.
[8] Moon, Crane and Matten, "Can corporations be citizens?" 434.
[9] Moon, Crane and Matten, "Can corporations be citizens?" 445.

Critical voices abound as well. In his 2012 book *Corporations are not people*, Clements makes the argument that corporations cannot be regarded as persons endowed with free speech because they cannot be punished the same way a "natural" person can be upon committing a crime – with a "combination of jail time, shame and repentance."[10] But if campaign contributions are free speech, then fines paid by a corporation represent speech that is taken away from them – it is money that a corporation could have used to advance a point of view, money that is no longer available. The corporation, therefore, is prevented from speaking – or has a portion of its free speech confiscated – as a consequence of wrongdoing, the same way that convicted felons are prevented from taking part in the civic life of the community for the duration of their sentence. The currency in which the former pays its dues is money, while the latter does so in time spent in prison. Just because one cannot inflict tangible, physical pain – i.e. incarceration – onto a corporation the same way that one can with regards to a convicted individual, it does not mean that the consequence of admitting to wrongdoing is not ultimately the same for corporations and individuals, namely absence from the community life.

Openly embracing the "concession" theory which sees corporations as existing at the pleasure of the state, Jeffrey Clements – speaking throughout the book in the plural form of the first person, as if he were standing as the sole representative of the human race against the alien corporations – harks back to "a longstanding American principle of guarding against concentrated corporate power that might overwhelm the larger interests of the nation."[11] To Clements and others like him, the interests of corporations are distinct from the interests of the individual citizens – so much that they could never meet – and as a result, the corporation needs to be pushed back into the state of a "*public tool* of economic policy." One could argue the case that the Honorable East India Trading Company, acting between the 17th and the 19th centuries, with its monopoly of trade in India, was a public tool of the English economy. State monopolies are indeed tools of economic policy – but ineffective ones, as the Soviet experiment has gravely shown. Private corporations, by comparison, activating in a free market, have historically created the most wealth than any other group of economic actors and have raised the standard of living to the same extent. One can plainly see today that wherever private companies were allowed to operate freely, wealth followed. Eastern Europe, South America, Africa and much of Asia, despite having incomparably richer natural resources and a much larger workforce, lagged behind Western Europe and North

---

[10] Jeffrey Clements, *Corporations are not people: Why they have more rights that you do and what you can do about it* (San Francisco: Barrett-Koehler, 2012): p. 81.

[11] Clements, *Corporations are not people*, 21.

America exactly for this reason, lacking innovation and stability due to the whims of tyrants or single Parties.

And yet, to Clements and other critics, corporations are the embodiment of greed and corruption, alien organizations that only serve themselves and damn millions of people to poverty and suffering for the sake of profit. But how long would such a corporation last in the public, globalized market of today, in which an offensive hoodie sold on the US and UK websites of H&M leads to the destruction of company shops in South Africa and large portions of lost revenue, in which an ad campaign prompts people to set fire to the company's products, like in the case of Nike and Kaepernick? It remains all too easy for authors and commentators to damn large corporations for seeking profit and perverting the otherwise morally righteous and economically pastoral human society, thus continuing through a different kind of language a popular and *populist* trend among intellectuals since the Middle Ages – that of attacking the rich for being rich.

Heaping blame onto corporations is indeed a popular sport in contemporary times. They are blamed for the existence of smoking,[12] pollution,[13] declining civic participation,[14] obesity,[15] teenage insecurity[16] and depression.[17] These attacks absolve individual people of all guilt but also agency, working with the same deterministic force and logic that any well-rounded conspiracy theory does, by externalizing any and all negative traits, intentions and actions to a separate entity that may as well be a racial, ethnic, sexual or economic group.

Following this logic, it is by no means an individual's fault that he or she smokes – it is the fault of Phillip Morris for selling cigarettes. It is by no means an individual's fault that he or she is overweight – it is the fault of McDonald's

---

[12] Liza Gross, "Smoke Screen: Big Vape is copying Big Tobacco's playbook," *The Verge*, November 16th, 2017, https://www.theverge.com/2017/11/16/16658358/vape-lobby-vaping-health-risks-nicotine-big-tobacco-marketing.

[13] Frank Jacobs, "Climate change: 100 CEOs killing the planet," *Big Think*, May 6th, 2019, https://bigthink.com/strange-maps/climate-change.

[14] Richard Moser, "How Corporate Power Killed Democracy," *CounterPunch*, December 6th, 2017, https://www.counterpunch.org/2017/12/06/how-corporate-power-killed-democracy/.

[15] Jacques Peretti, "Fat profits: how the good industry cashed in on obesity", *The Guardian*, August 7th, 2013, accessed November 21st 2019, https://www.theguardian.com/lifeandstyle/2013/aug/07/fat-profits-food-industry-obesity.

[16] Jeffrey Clements, *Corporations are not people*, 31.

[17] Terry Gross, "How Drug Companies Helped Shape a Shifting, Biological view of Mental Illness," *NPR*, May 2nd, 2019, https://www.npr.org/sections/health-shots/2019/05/02/718744068/how-drug-companies-helped-shape-a-shifting-biological-view-of-mental-illness.

and Coca-Cola for selling hamburgers and soda, despite numerous other reasons for which obesity is a stringent problem today. In the case of obesity in particular, McAllister et al. review "microorganisms, epigenetics, increasing maternal age, greater fecundity among people with higher adiposity, assortative mating, sleep debt, endocrine disruptors, pharmaceutical iatrogenesis, reduction in variability of ambient temperatures, and intrauterine and intergenerational effects as contributing factors to the obesity epidemic" as opposed to the "two most commonly advanced reasons for the increase in the prevalence of obesity," namely "certain food marketing practices and institutionally-driven reductions in physical activity." The same study notes that these commonly advanced reasons are popular because of their simplicity and because they "appeal to a prevalent anti-corporate sentiment."[18]

Similarly, it is not the fault of the individual who becomes inebriated and then violent towards his family – it is the fault of Heineken for selling beer, and so on. This overbearing and paternalistic approach to the individual is necessarily joined by a cry for state intervention.

Lacking any faith in the individual American consumer, authors like Clements clamor for state intervention against the devious profit-seeking companies that seek to poison the water and get children addicted to cigarettes. By contrast, the present book argues that the empowered, free speech-endowed corporations, will, in order to obtain profit, serve individuals – as consumers, not citizens – by catering to their wishes, just as they do when they design their products, and by respecting their social values in the political realm, influencing state institutions in accordance with the same wishes and values. The new corporate overlords will offer positive freedom – freedom *to* – to their consumers, but also negative freedom – freedom *from* – in order to retain them. As such, consumers will be free to boycott, just as they are now, in order to transmit an immediate political or social message to the corporations, which then will be able to exert its enormous *Citizens United* given influence in order to satisfy its consumers, just as an elected representative would. Corporations would be superior representatives in this respect, however, as any signal sent by the consumers would be visible in the profit books, incentivizing Coca-Cola, Gillette, Pepsi, Heineken, Barilla to act, if they still want to make money.

Clements rejects that artificial persons could ever be comparable in their behavior to natural ones, maintaining that "corporations are incapable of

---

[18] Nick Crossley, "Global anti-corporate struggle: a preliminary analysis," *Br J Sociol* 53, 4 (December 2002): pp. 667–691 doi: 10.1080/0007131022000021542.

virtue not because they are bad but because they are mere tools."[19] Indeed, corporations can be thought of as morally blank, with the values of their founders serving as a primary tool of orienting themselves socially, just as children take after the example of their parents when taking their first steps in the community. Such inclinations can be either encouraged or discouraged. Corporations can be taught to be virtuous by consumer choices. One's bag of groceries will, therefore, say more about one's values than the vote. By buying the products of a corporation that runs sweatshops and thrives in the corruption of less developed parts of the globalized world, an individual consumer will signal his support for such policies – with the opposite being equally true.

Another outlook taken on corporations aims to make them similar to the legal entity most associated by historians with modernity – the state. The attempt to democratize corporations through the concept of citizenship dates back to 1982, during the debates surrounding a new labor law in France. The corporation, an effective economic actor, was supposed to become similar to a state and subjected to democratization, with its top managers and executives put in contact with the realities of the workers. Alain Supiot, author of 2001 book *Beyond Employment. Changes in Work and the Future of Labor Law in Europe*, argues that these new, democratic corporations cannot be limited in goal to the amassing of profits for their directors and shareholders. Instead, coupling political with economic equality, they should follow the institutional formats of legitimate states, with the executive, legislative and judicial powers of the state equated to the employer's regulatory and disciplinary attributes.[20]

However, Supiot maintains a clear distinction between state and corporation, arguing that while the former covers all aspects of public life, "from birth to death," the corporation is limited to producing certain goods or supplying certain services. Moreover, the staff of a company cannot be identified as a people, as a company can disappear at any time. Instead, they form a "collective" that operates within an "archipelago of distinct legal entities."[21] Supiot's left-leaning remedy to the ills of corporate democracy is to break up the economic power of corporations, to re-empower the labor movement through workers' committees and to increase the state's economic role through nationalizations or "systematic intervention in the economy."

History has proven Supiot wrong. Corporations are not only increasingly influencing more aspects of public life – economy, politics, transport, health,

---

[19] Jeffrey Clements, *Corporations are not people*, 85.
[20] Thibault Le Texier, "Interview of author and professor Alain Supiot," Espirit, April 13th, 2018, https://www.eurozine.com/economic-democracy-interview-alain-supiot/.
[21] Le Texier, "Interview of author and professor Alain Supiot."

lifestyle, entertainment, representation, research – they are also increasingly becoming identified with certain beliefs, groups of people and social goals, representing an evolutionary step from the profit-seeking company, while retaining the same fundamental goal of maximizing profits.

Moreover, companies can no longer be seen as subjects of the state's power and will, as they have traversed borders, with brands and funds impacting communities all over the globe, and have attained a personhood that is detached from the will of any manager, CEO or group of shareholders, being instead primarily dependent on its consumers. If Winkler is to be believed, the evolution of the company as a person – the essential crossing from *union of persons* to *person* – was a lie, but that matters little now, just as so many episodes of history do not matter to the states today.

As befitting their involvement in the political sphere, corporations have also seen more and more calls for control – specifically, democratic control – over their own actions. Because companies have become more than profit-seeking economic endeavors, and have transformed into social actors with political positions, a new theoretical grasp on their existence is indeed needed, and democracy-through-shareholders seems to be one method. Large, stock-based corporations are privately owned and managed, but as great giants, they are separated in two - CEOs and managers handle the head while the money they spend and the profits they make go to the body, the investors, which refrain from becoming involved in the day-to-day. Executive and public, representative and represented, managers and shareholders – the logic is similar, but if corporations are to act as states-within-states, artificial persons that are more than the sum of their collective shareholders, it means that they are accountable to only a fraction of the public, their shareholders.

As such, corporate legitimacy in the political sphere is questionable. How is a professionalized, non-accountable actor to take a major role in the democratic process without itself being democratic in functioning? Hart and Zingales ask an apparently simple question – "if a consumer is willing to spend $100 more to reduce pollution, why would that consumer not want a company he or she holds shares in to do this too?"[22] Their argument is that the 100 million Americans that invest in the stock market should be *represented* by the corporations in which they invest, their views and opinions taken into account, and that profit should not be the ultimate goal of companies. The way to do that, following the authors, is to allow shareholders broader powers through voting within corporations. They quote the privatization campaigns initiated

---

[22] Oliver Hart and Luigi Zingales, "Companies should maximize shareholder welfare not market value," *Journal of Law, Finance and Accounting* 2, 2 (2017): pp. 247-274.

by Margaret Thatcher in the United Kingdom, thought in a way so as to involve people in the running of businesses in order for them to defend the market economy.

However, the two authors concede that when market value and shareholder value are divorced, even the smallest shareholder, employing rational behavior, will prefer market value. At the same time, shareholder-democracy seems now a distant ideal, as investment companies and various technocrats make most of the decisions within a corporation.[23] Hart and Zingales rightly hold that "most shareholders have a mix of financial goals and ethical beliefs...the profit-hungry firm can be part of a system that satisfies both their desires."[24] However, in the formulation of their plebiscitary capitalism, the two do not consider that market value may become dependent, in some domains of economic activity, on a form of societal implication by the same corporations, and that some segments of the consumer base, enjoying a choice of nearly interchangeable products, will naturally drift towards the products of the corporation that is most similar to their beliefs. Moreover, not unlike numerous critics, they focus on the people running the company, and do not take the *Citizens United* decision into account, as their scope is hardly political.

Evidence showing that individuals look to companies to stand as representatives of their values piles on with every political scandal. When the family separation policy enacted by the United States Immigrations and Customs Enforcement agency enraged segments of the American society, workers from the biggest tech companies in the country – Salesforce, Microsoft, Amazon and Google – demanded that their employers cut ties with the border guards and other agencies. In continuation to the progressive idealism of the early West Coast, such businesses often proclaimed their liberal values. If Google started with the motto "don't be evil," Salesforce CEO Marc Benioff often reminded people of his company's dedication to equality for sexual minorities and gender pay equity, threatening, in one episode to stop doing business within Georgia if the state legislature passed a law permitting discrimination against the LGBTQ community.[25]

---

[23] "What if the unwashed masses got to vote on companies' strategies?" *The Economist*, November 30th, 2017, https://www.economist.com/business/2017/11/30/what-if-the-unwashed-masses-got-to-vote-on-companies-strategies.

[24] "What if the unwashed masses got to vote on companies' strategies?" https://www.economist.com/business/2017/11/30/what-if-the-unwashed-masses-got-to-vote-on-companies-strategies.

[25] Laura Sydell, "Tech Workers Demand CEOs Stop Doing Business with ICE, Other U.S. Agencies", *NPR*, July 14th, 2018, https://www.npr.org/2018/07/14/628765208/tech-workers-demand-ceos-stop-doing-business-with-ice-other-u-s-agencies.

Other authors sense the issue at hand more acutely. In her talk at the 2001 CIBAM Global Business Colloquium, Noreena Hertz highlighted low voter turnout and falling party membership everywhere in the developed world, concluding that "never has the currency of the vote been so discredited." Instead of voting, Hertz argues that

> [...] the most effective way to be political today is not cast your vote at the ballot box but to do so at the supermarket or at a shareholder's meeting. Why? Because corporations respond. While governments dithered about the health value of GM foods, supermarkets faced with consumer unrest pulled the products off their shelves overnight. While nations spoke about ethical foreign policy, it was corporations who actually pulled out of Burma rather than risk censure by their customers. When stories broke over the world of children sewing footballs for Reebok and Nike for a pittance, what did governments do about it? Nothing, whereas corporations stepped in with innovative plans for dealing with the child labor problem. Delivering a quality product at a reasonable cost is not all that is now demanded of corporations. The key to consumer satisfaction is not only how well a company treats its customers, but increasingly whether it is perceived to be taking its responsibilities to society seriously. [...] Consumer politics is the new politics, and politicians are stepping aside to make space so that consumers can become to an ever-greater extent agents of political change.[26]

Hertz's forceful defense of consumer activism and corporate responsiveness and involvement in the political realm has been validated time and time again, and it is becoming, as chapter IX will demonstrate, the rule rather than the exception. Driven by market appeal, Hertz's corporations are the opposite of the giants that push a private, investor or CEO-based, minority-oriented agenda. Instead, she argues that "minority interests or unattractive causes may well get pushed aside"[27] not by the greed of the corporations but by the majoritarian, consumer-driven trends to which they will be subjected. Amoral vehicles following whatever road will grant them a higher profit, Hertz argues that corporations cannot be a full replacement for the state for they are not endowed with ethics, and will at times be taken over by interests that will not coincide with those of the society – but cannot the same be said about the state?

---

[26] Noreena Hertz, "Better to shop than to vote?" *Business Ethics: A European Review* 10, 3 (2001): pp. 190-193 https://doi.org/10.1111/1467-8608.00232.
[27] Hertz, "Better to shop than to vote?" 192.

How many times have the institutions of the state turned against the citizens in a genocidal frenzy, spurred on by the intended goal of killing as many of them as possible? Can the same be said about corporations? Of course not – even in the savage days of early capitalism, when children worked in mines and grueling work days shortened lifespans, corporations did not start with the intention of killing, and any tragic loss of life was, of no less blame, collateral to the pursuit of profit.

In 2018, when protesters showed up – not in front of a governmental agency with regulatory power, but in front of the Salesforce headquarters in San Francisco – the tech company was prompted to deny any ties to ICE.[28] A few months later, a Salesforce donation was refused by an NGO on the grounds of the company's connection to the government, adding to the pressure created by the 650 employees who signed a petition asking Salesforce to live up to its values. Workers protesting their employer for the sake of values, not wages or working conditions, is a new reality of the politically involved companies. In the past, scientists and engineers refused to work with their employer due to similar reasons – after the bombs were dropped in Hiroshima and Nagasaki. The employer, however, was the United States government, and not a tech company in California.

Clearly, while democracy-through-companies is not yet a reality, the issue of representation cannot be denied. Employees and consumers today expect their employers and the companies they support through the buying of products – an act which can freely be considered speech – to be like them, to protect the planet, fight injustice, tackle sexism and to stand for what they stand. They see corporations as their representatives. However, to be a representative, one needs to be a person, not only in a strictly legal sense, but in a political one as well.

The next chapter builds on the ruling in *Citizens United* and argues that speaking makes politics possible, and that any person who can speak can therefore engage in politics. This means that with *Citizens United*, "natural" persons are joined by "artificial" persons in the realm of politics – again, a formalization of already existing, albeit insufficiently codified or acknowledged state of being, as chapter IX will show.

---

[28] Makena Kelly, "Immigration nonprofit refuses $250,000 Salesforce donation over its contract with US government," *The Verge*, July 19th, 2018, https://www.theverge.com/2018/7/19/17590240/immigration-non-profit-raices-refuses-salesforce-donation.

Chapter VI

Political Personhood

Ever since the most stellar minds in the city-states of ancient Greece pondered upon the best possible way to organize human life, one element remained constant – the individuals, the humans themselves. *Zoon politikon*, subjects to a God-anointed king, equal citizens of a republic and finally rational voters, men and women have remained the one common feature of philosophy and political science. When one talks about politics, one talks about ideas, feats, feelings and opinions but most of all, about people. Whether it is the one who rules or the many, to borrow Aristotle's separation of political regimes, they are all people.

Despite the so far unchallenged status that humans enjoyed in all matters political, questions regarding the best form of governance still linger, even if democracy, for all its faults, remains the best system drawn up to date. Man, however, is about to be dethroned as the principal political actor in the world. It is, poetically, something of his making that yearns to replace him – the corporation.

A separation must be made before moving forward. Evidently, not all companies are not politically-active and socially-aware, nor are they all incentivized to act as representatives of their consumers – not to the same extent, at least. The influences under which a large multinational with interests, assets and relations spanning across continents are very different from those that are being laid on a neighborhood corner shop. A useful method by which to grasp this separation is exactly by considering personhood in a more – for lack of a better word – *personal* way. Simply put, if an employee can narrow down the fact that his or her superior's wishes and decisions are the driving force of the entire enterprise, then the company is probably too small to be counted among those discussed in this book. If one can answer the question "who do you work for?" with another's name, the same rule applies. Large multinational corporations, on the other hand, cannot be pinned down to a single person's – or a group's – wishes and decision, be they the CEO, the board of directors, the majority shareholders and so on. Coca-Cola is not James Quincey, its CEO since 2017 and a man about which most people will never hear – it is Coca-Cola. It is the brand. It is the people who buy it every day. As inventive as marketing departments are, they cannot imbue a corporation with an identity, for that identity can be easily rejected by consumers, as chapter IX will plainly demonstrate.

In 2010, the United States Supreme Court ruled in *Citizens United v. Federal Election Commission*, stating that according to the First Amendment, the government had no right to restrict expenditures for campaign ads supporting or even attacking candidates by corporations, associations and labor unions so long as the money is not directly given to the politicians. In this case, the conservative NGO *Citizens United* argued that airing a film critical of Hillary Clinton, then-candidate for the Democratic nomination for presidency in 2008, is within its rights. The final decision of the court effectively meant that corporations could contribute as much as they deemed necessary to a certain campaign based on their inherent freedom of speech.[1]

Citizens United, as the case informally became known, is the latest in a line of cases that expanded the category of personhood from "simply" natural persons to corporations, unions, and other legal entities. By legal means, *Citizens United* forces political philosophy to once again look at the foundations of political philosophy and ask what a person is in terms of natural and political rights.

Political personhood, as political scientists have come to understand it, is a status that allows a person to exercise the range of constitutional rights connected to persons, and it entitles a person to receive the constitutional protections that accompany those rights,[2] the two parts reunited making, as Ellis calls it, a "tiered personhood." Following Hobbes as well, a distinction can be made between "natural" and "artificial" persons. While he defined the representative as an artificial person, Hobbes also gave a broader definition of personhood – "a person is a thing that we may observe speaking words or performing actions."[3] Speaking, therefore, is part of the essence of what means to be a person – we recognize each other as rational, thinking, coherent and *human* by speaking to one another. In the absence of speech, any political way of organizing of a community would be impossible, biblically depicted by the story of tower of Babel.

Leaving tiered personhood aside, one can already deduce a basic premise – entities must be recognized and formally categorized in order to be allocated

---

[1] Kirk Ludwig, "Corporate Speech in Citizens United vs. Federal Election Commission," *Spazio Filosofico* (2016) pp. 1-33 https://www.spaziofilosofico.it/en/numero-16/6059/corporate-speech-in-citizens-united-vs-federal-election-commission/.

[2] Atiba R. Ellis, "Citizens United and Tiered Personhood," *The John Marshall Law Review* 44, 3 (November 2011): pp. 12-33.

[3] Thomas Hobbes, *Leviathan*, Project Gutenberg E-Books, https://www.gutenberg.org/files/3207/3207-h/3207-h.htm#link2H_4_0048.

their due rights. This process is often taken for granted by the shared contemporary legal understanding when it comes to natural persons, i.e. humans. The same procedure was and still is utilized every time a right is conferred or confirmed by a court or in a legal document. For example, before being conferred, the civil, political and social rights described by Marshall[4] had to recognize those to whom they applied and therefore, the need for a definition of political personhood was formulated and hence perpetually accepted by courts in every legal process.[5] Simply put, each time an individual appears before a court, no matter in which capacity, the court formally recognizes him or her as a "natural" person – *a human being.*

As the judicial framework evolved together with modernity, political personhood found its stronger political avatar in the notion of citizenship. It is the citizen who votes, stands for election, files petitions, organizes political groups, occupies an office and eventually affects the laws of a country, together with a larger group of voters. However, this straightforward concept itself proved problematic and idealistic to a certain degree and was deemed distant from reality by political science scholars. Hegelian pluralism, in which the individual is protected by his associations "so that their eternal vigilance and not simply his own is the price of his liberty," was one answer.[6] For Hegel, smaller groups dispersed and shared the cost of citizenship while organically enhancing self-determination through participation. Pluralism, together with its addendum of political individualism based on unalienable rights, has been, in turn, named the liberal answer to Marxist theory. However, Waltzer suggests that the American answer to Marx is not pluralism, but passivity and privatization. It is in the U.S. that corporations, growing out of these two features, became "politically self-aware," that is, aware of their own interests, individuality, the existence of other corporations within the market and finally, their possibilities of participation in the regulatory capacity. As it has been shown in chapter I, corporations of the 1920s were already readily impacting policy-making, while numerous "natural persons" lived at the edges of the political community, unable to impact even the smallest cog in the political machine that ruled their lives.

To what degree is citizenship tied to actual political activity? Following Waltzer, there are three kinds of citizens: a) the oppressed citizen whose obligations depend upon the ways in which he chooses and manages to involve

---

4 T.H. Marshall, *Citizenship and Social Class* (New York: Cambridge University Press, 1950): pp. 1-47.
5 Ellis, "Citizens United," 2-5.
6 Michael Waltzer, *Obligations. Essays on Disobedience, War and Citizenship* (Cambridge and London: Harvard University Press, 1982): pp. 202-218.

himself in the larger community; b) the alienated citizen who does not participate at all in political life because he chooses not to and thinks of the state as an alien under whose jurisdiction he peacefully wants to live; and finally c) the pluralist citizen who shares in ruling and being ruled because of his plural membership to smaller groups. His citizenship is fully accepted only by joining other groups which fall into one of two categories: groups that are actually making claims against the state or groups that are not putting forward such claims.[7]

Corporations can be divided in the same fashion as citizens. According to their influence, interest and reach, they make claims against the state or not. Moreover, as we see most evidently in the American case, corporations divide themselves according to their area of activity and collectively make claims against the state through lobbying. For example, the pharmaceutical/health products lobby, the largest one, represents the interest of 338 clients such as Pfizer Inc., Amgen Inc., the Biotechnology Innovations Organization, etc., and employs 1300 lobbyists. The pharmaceutical lobby is followed by the insurance lobby, the electric utilities group, the business associations group, oil and gas and so on, including even a TV/Movie/Music industry lobby. All of these corporations, associations of corporations and their subsequent lobby groups have been tremendously empowered politically by the *Citizens United* ruling.

In their actions as vessels of political personhood, corporations have had incomparably more success than "natural" citizens. Innumerable laws have been written and passed with special consultation provided by experts paid by corporations; lobbies have saved perhaps billions in tax breaks so far, and elected representatives could always be reached more easily by companies than by the regular citizen, providing for a much shorter and effective communications channel. If it has become clear that corporations are, by all means and purposes, more active, informed and effective citizens, they are also better representatives of their consumers and closer to them than the distant elected officials.

This chapter has connected citizenship and political personhood with the "artificial" persons that are the politically-engaged corporations and companies. Through lobbying, corporations have long been able to take part in drafting legislation. Through their free speech, endowed to them by the US Supreme Court, corporations can now also *speak* on certain political and social matters. They can, therefore, take part in the political life of the city. They can more directly legislate, represent and advance demands. The next chapter will fill in the other actors within a political system – the political parties.

---

[7] Waltzer, *Obligations. Essays on Disobedience, War and Citizenship*, 202-218.

Chapter VII

Parties, Corporations and Representation

Modern-day mass democracy is a political system that revolves around institutions and parties. While the first provide the framework by which a society functions, it is the second which recruits the people who populate and lead these institutions. Moreover, it is the parties that act as a liaison between the citizenry and the apparatus of government, translating the desires and needs of the people as inputs and feeding them into the bureaucratic machine of the democratic state. In order to fulfill that role, parties and elected officials need to be accepted by society as representative and trusted as capable to enact change. However, as an NPR/PBS poll from January 2018 shows, 54% of Americans have little or no confidence in the presidency. Similarly, 71% of all American adults had the same to say about Congress, with the Republican and Democratic parties faring just as bad in matters of trust themselves.[1] Party identification in the United States since 2004 has also plateaued at 60%, most of the time averaging in the 50s.[2] Party membership, in turn, is low in most democracies around the world.

At the same time, a survey conducted by the Georgetown University and New York University in 2018 showed that while partisan affiliation affected the way in which people viewed the state of the American democracy, Americans overall have lost confidence in the institutions of their country. As such, the top-ranking institutions were: the military, followed by Amazon, Google, local police and colleges and universities. At the bottom, one could find the press, the executive branch, Facebook, political parties and Congress.[3] Democracy rests on institutions and parties – but people have lost trust in either, steering away from the political sphere and mistrusting any government initiative as subservient to special interests. Americans, on the other hand, seem to trust

---

[1] "NPR/PBS NewsHour/Marist Poll Results, January 2018," Maristpoll, accessed February 10th 2019, www.maristpoll.marist.edu, accessed on the 10th of February 2019.

[2] "Party Affiliation," *Gallup*, accessed February 11th 2019, https://news.gallup.com/poll/15370/party-affiliation.aspx.

[3] Jonathan M. Ladd, Joshua A. Tucker & Sean Kates. "2018 American Institutional Confidence: The Health of American Democracy in an era of hyper-polarization." Baker Center for Leadership & Governance, accessed December 3rd, 2019, http://aicpoll.com.

some corporations more than their government[4] – certainly more than political parties. But does trust entail communication and representation?

Representation, Hanna Pitkin starts off, means the making present of something which is nevertheless not literally present. The suggestion probably most familiar from the literature on representation is that the representative must do what his principal would do, must act as if the principal himself were acting (making-the-represented-present). This, however, presents problems. These problems have been most clearly formulated within the mandate-independence debate, which can be summarized as such: should a representative do what his constituents want, and be bound by mandates or instructions from them; or should he be free to act as seems best to him in pursuit of their welfare?[5]

Pitkin takes what is valid from both theories: the representative must have some freedom, otherwise he is a tool, and at the same time he cannot be persistently at odds with the desires of his constituency. If he is, we think of him as a separate being acting on his own to pursue his own goals. Modern Parliaments all over the world reject the imperative mandate, which transforms the representative into a servant catering exclusively to his constituents, and award elected officials a wider range of freedom – which does not save them from being accountable to the voters at every electoral cycle.

What is the place of corporations in this framework? If one is to accept the reality of the market as a daily plebiscite, he should also accept the fact that it is governed by the moment-to-moment choices made by consumers. It is they who decide, by simply following their individual interest, which company is to thrive and which to fail. It is the desires of the consumers which make it possible for an apparently insignificant local challenger to face off against a huge multinational. According to Sowell, whenever one refers to "the market," he refers to "a set of conditions in which individuals make their own choices in

---

[4] Americans' trust in corporations did not falter even in front of the coronavirus pandemic. In the summer of 2020, an Axios/Harris poll revealed that around 75% of consumers thought that "companies were more reliable than the federal government in keeping America running." Grocers like Kroger or Publix, delivery companies Fedex, UPS or Amazon, packaged goods companies like Procter & Gamble, streaming companies like Netflix and pharmacies like Walgreens and CVS topped the trust levels in the poll, while social media giants, airline and telecom companies were placed at the bottom. Sara Fischer, "Axios Harris Poll 100: Corporate trust soars during the pandemic," *Axios*, July 30th 2020, https://www.axios.com/coronavirus-clorox-amazon-disney-groceries-public-approval-bb24d50c-f77a-4e2e-ac2e-3760123b8755.html?utm_source=newsletter&utm_medium=email&utm_campaign=newsletter_axiosam&stream=top.

[5] Hanna Fenichel Pitkin, *The Concept of Representation* (Berkeley: University of California Press, 1967).

light of their own respective values."[6] In this respect, the economic and political markets are no different.

What one knows as capitalism would therefore be better described as "consumerism" – a term long muddied by the opponents of the free market but which in reality describes an economy coordinated by prices where "those with the most knowledge of their own particular situation to make bids for goods and resources based on that knowledge, rather than on their ability to influence other people."[7] Economists have argued for decades that as producers struggle to satisfy the highest number of people, their products become similar, indistinguishable. The same trend can be found in mainstream politics, where the chase for the "median voter" leads the left and the right toward a common center.

In the last years, however, another reality has disproven these longstanding ideas in both economics and politics. Most conspicuously, a resurgence of radicalism at the heart of the "West" – the United States and Great Britain – led figures such as Donald Trump and Jeremy Corbyn to positions of power. It is only recently that political moves taking actors away from the center have resulted in electoral success.

Similarly, while companies and corporations are forced by the forces of competition to maintain their products within a high degree of similarity, they have employed another method of differentiating themselves from their competitors – political orientation and value identification. This strategy rests on what Hanna Pitkin labels "descriptive representation." According to the view of descriptive representation, true representation requires that the legislature be so selected that its composition corresponds accurately to that of the whole nation. Supporters of this view include John Adams, partly Edmund Burke and Sidney and Beatrice Webb. Descriptive representation is also the concept serving as a foundation for the feminism push for gender quotas.

However, the descriptive representation of the values of consumers is now employed by corporations, which stand to gain if they identify themselves with the values of larger groups of consumers. If the products a company puts forth are indistinguishable from those of the competition, the consumer needs to be convinced by other methods to choose a particular brand. As a result, *companies must become more like their consumers, politically, if they are to survive and thrive on the product-saturated free market.*

---

[6] Thomas Sowell, *Basic Economics: A Citizen's Guide to the Economy* (New York: Perseus Books, 2000): 308.

[7] Sowell, *Basic Economics*, 14.

A few examples more than clarify the recent trend. In the aftermath of the white supremacist rally in Charlottesville, Virginia, in the summer of 2017, people attending the rally started being identified and subsequently fired from their place of employment. In one case, in a statement that was released by the president of Mojo Burrito, a fast-food company, upon firing the employee Terrence Hightower, it was made clear that the company itself "does not condone harassment, racism or discrimination of any kind."[8] Similarly, Limehouse & Sons, a construction company based in South Carolina, fired Nigel Krofta for taking part in the rally. Cole White, another participant in the Charlottesville rally, resigned from Berkeley-based restaurant Top Dog, while public workers identified at the march were placed on administrative leave or forced to apologize.

Why would Mojo Burrito and all other companies fire Terrance Hightower and the likes for attending a march? Their role is to serve the consumers on the market with high quality and low-cost products, not to represent values and beliefs that can immediately be identified as moral or outright political. However, that is exactly what these companies had to do, even independently of the wishes of their owners, in order to ensure their economic survival.

Another case was that of Patagonia and REI, recreational gear companies that criticized President Trump's decision to reduce the size of Bears Ears and Grand Staircase-Escalante National Monuments by nearly 2 million acres combined. Patagonia, a longstanding activist for the protection of the environment, urged people to protest the decision.[9] Many more examples of companies and corporations assuming a political stance make the news. Barilla, the world's leading pasta-making company, was boycotted after its chairman said it would only portray "classic families" – meaning heterosexual couples – in its ads.[10] As a primary channel of information sharing, Facebook has long been an important medium for political action. With its recent push against "trolls" who take advantage of the algorithms, the company has had its employees

---

[8] Naomi LaChance, "More Nazis Are Getting Identified And Fired After Charlottesville," *Huffington Post*, August 16th, 2017, https://www.huffpost.com/entry/more-nazis-are-getting-identified-and-fired-after-charlottesville_b_599477dbe4b0eef7ad2c0318.

[9] Travis Andrews, "The President Stole Your Land': Patagonia, REI Blast Trump On National Monument Rollbacks," *The Washington Post*, December 5th, 2017, https://www.washingtonpost.com/news/morning-mix/wp/2017/12/05/the-president-stole-your-land-patagonia-rei-blast-trump-on-national-monument-rollbacks/.

[10] Lizzy Davies, "Pasta Firm Barilla Boycotted Over 'Classic Family' Remarks," *The Guardian*, September 26th, 2013, https://www.theguardian.com/world/2013/sep/26/pasta-firm-barilla-boycott-gay.

accompany government workers, even providing technical assistance to candidates.[11]

A push for a more politically involved corporate world came early on. Writing to Eugene Sydnor, Chairman of the Education Committee of the United States Chamber of Commerce, two months before he was nominated, United States Supreme Court Justice Lewis Powell made the demand in 1971. Noticing a "massive attack" on free-market capitalism from communists and New Leftists, Justice Powell also deplored the "apathy of business." The traditional role of business, Powell noted, was not to combat propaganda, but to produce. However, he charged them with a new responsibility – that of ensuring the survival of the free enterprise system. According to the Justice, "the day is long past when the chief executive officer of a major corporation discharges his responsibility by maintaining a satisfactory growth of profits." Instead, public relations and governmental affairs should be a key domain of activity for business managers and businesses themselves, although, writing in 1971, Powell deemed that the influence of business in politics was rather weak – decrying "the impotency of business."[12]

Taking the decade between the mid-1960s to the mid-1970s as a timeline, Vogel set out in his 1983 article in order to assess the thesis according to which businesses exert massive amounts of influence in the American society. One – and the author himself does so – might argue that the period in time chosen by Vogel could not have been worse for businesses in the United States – the Berkeley protests started in 1964, signaling, along with the wider movement opposing the Vietnam War, that individual citizens were banding together and expressing themselves on an ideological level, most often in terms that were adversarial toward established institutions, in a way that the 2019 American society does not witness. Vogel dully notes that "[...]in spite of corporate opposition [...] between 1965 and 1975 more than twenty-five major pieces of federal regulatory legislation in the areas of consumer and environmental protection, occupational health and safety and personnel policy were enacted by the Federal Government."[13] What gives corporations power over the political

---

[11] Lauren Etter, Vernon Silver and Sarah Frier, "How Facebook's Political Unit Enables the Dark Art of Digital Propaganda," Bloomberg, December 21st, 2017, https://www.bloom berg.com/news/features/2017-12-21/inside-the-facebook-team-helping-regimes-that-reach-out-and-crack-down.

[12] Lewis F. Powell Jr., "Confidential Memorandum – Attack on American Free Enterprise System," *Washington and Lee University Scholarly Commons*, accessed June 3rd, 2018, https://scholarlycommons.law.wlu.edu/powellmemo/.

[13] David Vogel, "The Power of Business in America: A Re-appraisal," British Journal of Political Science 13, 1 (January 1983): pp. 23-24.

discourse and agenda in the United States? Put simply, persuasion. According to Vogel, "business is in a uniquely privileged position to persuade the public that the satisfaction of its demands is essential if high growth rates are to be restored."[14] No other political – or potentially political - actor underpins the history, wealth and society in the United States. As Ayn Rand put it,

> Businessmen are the only group that distinguishes capitalism and the American way of life from the totalitarian statism that is swallowing the rest of the world. All the other social groups – workers, farmers, professional men, scientists, soldiers – exist under dictatorships, even though they exist in chains, in terror, in misery, and in progressive self-destruction. But there is no such group as businessmen under a dictatorship.[15]

The newfound influence of businesses, according to the letter written by Justice Powell, should be felt in university campuses, schools, among professors, media, scholarly journals, and so on. Secret until 1972, the document was rediscovered in the 1990s and made available to the public in 2000 by critics of the neoconservative movement and its connection to big businesses, as just another proof of the negative influence of the connection between politicians and businessmen.

The link, as this chapter has shown, goes well beyond the people in office or at the forefront of corporations, touching the very identity or essence of the companies themselves, and the relationship – at first, purely economic – between them and the consumers. The next chapter recounts dozens of episodes in which this link became visible, sometimes violently so, pitting consumers against corporations and corporations against elected officials such as the President of the United States. The clashes foretell of a brave new world in which corporations will have to be truer representatives of the people – now as consumers, not voters – than politicians and parties.

---

[14] Vogel, "The Power of Business in America: A Re-appraisal," 42.
[15] Ayn Rand, *Capitalism, The Unknown Ideal* (New York: Penguin Group, 1946), 38.

Chapter VIII

Partisan Industries and Campaign Contributions

The previous chapter has argued that corporations can serve as representatives of their consumers in front of the American political establishment, and noted how some corporations receive more trust than the major political parties. But corporations are also an unofficial part of governing. Indeed, the United States is unique due to the degree in which corporations can become involved in elections and even in the process of drafting legislation. Through lobby groups, foreign firms such as the Chinese e-commerce giant Alibaba can participate in the legislative act by ghostwriting bills which can then be sponsored in states all over the U.S.[1] This is common practice in an electoral system where a healthy campaign budget can mean an assured victory. One can conclude that in the U.S., *money speaks louder* than in other democratic systems.

At times, state legislators and lobbyists can even be reunited in nation-wide conventions and forums meant to hasten the same process of passing corporate-friendly laws. These private meetings are organized by lobbyists and their corporate backers with the aim of handing elected representatives from various states draft bills that can then be taken back and used as models by legislators from all over the United States. In this way, fast-food companies, tech giants, pharmaceutical developers and the energy sector can secure by proxy the prerogatives of a Congress, whose members are normally accountable to their voters and to none other, and for whose public, collective benefit they should govern. However, on issues such as minimum wage or waste disposal, the voices of corporations are louder, and their influence extends to a degree that is unimaginable even if one would compare them to a very large pressure group made out of individual, "natural" citizens. In this process, ideological leaning does not matter that much, seeing as corporations pursue tax breaks, profits-as-lack-of-taxation, not profits-as-sales, as they do in relation to consumers.

---

[1] Lee Fang and Nick Surgey, "Chinese corporation Alibaba joins group ghostwriting American laws," *The Intercept*, March 20th, 2018, https://theintercept.com/2018/03/20/alibaba-chinese-corporation-alibaba-joins-group-ghostwriting-american-laws/.

Why are corporations in the United States so involved in the process of drafting bills? One explanation would be that the government simply renounced the resources to do it. In 1995, a Republican majority in Congress led by Newt Gingrich started to defund the institution. Arguing that the federal budget was bloated due to the Washington bureaucracy, the Republicans left the state unable to draft complex legislation, sometimes amounting to thousands of pages, in a relatively short time. That ability was transferred to giant lobby firms, starting a very lucrative industry in the capital of the United States.[2] In this way, legislative deadlock was avoided by an understaffed Congress by delegating the ability to write legislation.

Table A – Source of funds by sector, 2015-2016 election cycle

Rank	Sector	Amount	To Cands/Parties	Dems	Repubs	To DEMS / To REPUBS
1	Finance/Insur/RealEst	$912,350,256	$465,411,328	42.2%	57.6%	
2	Other	$593,872,619	$494,067,188	58.3%	41.3%	
3	Ideology/Single-Issue	$411,670,519	$271,757,477	61.2%	38.7%	
4	Misc Business	$374,585,616	$267,396,042	43.2%	56.5%	
5	Communic/Electronics	$254,271,572	$159,533,487	67.3%	32.5%	
6	Health	$222,951,892	$165,365,804	49.7%	50.1%	
7	Lawyers & Lobbyists	$198,008,151	$184,822,173	68.4%	31.3%	
8	Energy/Nat Resource	$149,794,510	$97,886,669	22.2%	77.7%	
9	Labor	$142,121,291	$63,252,831	86.9%	12.9%	
10	Agribusiness	$93,418,018	$68,528,589	26.7%	72.8%	
11	Construction	$88,793,884	$66,993,474	31.2%	68.5%	
12	Transportation	$79,237,183	$63,393,786	30.1%	69.7%	
13	Defense	$25,873,898	$25,605,610	38.2%	61.6%	

Source: Center for Responsive Politics, https://www.opensecrets.org, accessed on December 20th 2017

It is possible, by analyzing the money invested by industries into lobbying and campaign financing, to attribute a political coloration or even orientation to corporations. However, the interests of corporations, sometimes championed by Democrats and sometimes by Republicans, can shift, immediately followed by their funds. As Table A shows, Democrats generally receive the backing of a

---

[2] Ryan Grim, "Elizabeth Warren unveils radical anti-corruption platform," *The Intercept*, August 21st, 2018, https://theintercept.com/2018/08/21/elizabeth-warren-unveils-radical-anti-corruption-platform/.

variety of economic actors, from law firms and labor unions to communication-electronics companies and single-issue pressure groups. Conversely, Republicans dominate the construction, energy, transportation and defense sectors, relatively holding the upper hand in other important sectors.

Table A might prove terrifying for some, revealing a world in which individuals are powerless beings, subjected to the whims of big industries that have not become politicized but that overtook the democratic political system, adopting and shaping the values of a political camp in order to advance their own interest.

Only in the year 2016, during the presidential elections, 2393 super PACs (Political Action Committees) raised a total of $1.79 billion, spending $1 billion directly. Out of the sum, $405 million were spent on ads attacking Republicans, compared to $285 million-worth of ads attacking Democrats. Conversely, $261 million were spent in support of Republicans, while only $104 million were spent for Democrats. Regardless of purpose, one fact is telling – 70% of the money spent in campaigns in 2016 was provided by the top 100 donors and 95% of the entire sum was given by 1% of donors, both individuals and organizations.[3]

Individual business conglomerates and corporations, acting through super PACs, could also directly make use of funds from their treasuries. Repeated million-dollar donations from the Koch Industries, Valero Services, Wheatland Tube, Mountaire Corp, Pilot Corp, Hillwood Development, the Chevron Corporation, Maratho Petroleum and NextEra Energy found their way to the vaults of conservative super PACs like the Senate Leadership Fund, the America First Action and the Congressional Leadership Fund, becoming available for Republican candidates throughout 2017 and 2018.[4]

The method of recognizing the political leanings of entire industries through the campaign contributions made by corporations active in each domain held up in 2018 as well. Non-industry groups, both Republican and Democratic, gathered hundreds of millions of dollars – most of them from organizations, not individuals. However, the securities & investment industry, coupled with the finance industry, made by far the largest donations to both conservatives and liberals, followed by the environment industry (Democratic), the

---

[3] "Super PACs: How Many Donors Give," OpenSecrets.org, Center for Responsive Politics, accessed March 15th 2019, https://www.opensecrets.org/outside-spending/donor-stats.
[4] "Corporate Contributions to Outside Groups," OpenSecrets.org, Center for Responsive Politics, accessed April 17th 2019, https://www.opensecrets.org/outsidespending/summ.php?chrt=V&type=S.

casino/gambling industry (Republican), the building trade unions (Democratic), the health services industry (Republican), the non-profit institutions (Democratic), the real estate industry (approximately even to both parties) and the manufacturing and distributing industry (Republican).[5] In total, in the 2018 electoral cycle of elections – congressional and gubernatorial – outside spending groups, mostly corporate-backed super PACs, spent $134 million in support of Republicans and $178.5 million in support of Democrats, but they also spent $379 million attacking Republicans and $354.8 million attacking Democrats.

However, the involvement of companies in the sphere of campaign contributions can be explain through the rational or Public Choice theory, just like that of individuals. In his 1957 treatise *An Economic Theory of Democracy*, Anthony Downs argued that the ideological proximity between elector and candidate determines the preference of the elector and therefore the outcome of the election. Such was the importance Downs gave to this principle that he called it the "fundamental determinant of a nation's politics." His theory became a framework for future models which continued to build upon it, all within the school of Public Choice. Thus, while the Davis-Himich-Ordeshook model stressed the vital importance of the "median voter," the perceptual model formulated by Himich and Pollard in 1981 identified the informative importance of the ideological "labels" – for example "liberal" or "conservative." Through such a label, the elector could obtain all the information he needed regarding the candidate's stance on numerous issues without having to bear the usual heavy cost – the influence of economy in this theory is evident – of getting informed.[6]

Palfrey added his own model, arguing that when – and only when – a segment of voters is left "unattended" by establishment-parties on either side of the political continuum, a new party may emerge. This web of public choice theories also takes into account the *psychological effect of the electoral system*, a duvergerian concept that describes a situation in which voters act strategically.

At first glance, we realize how anthropocentric Public Choice Theory, and indeed political science as a whole, has been ever since Aristotle distinguished "man" as a *zoon politikon*, a political animal that exists exclusively in the *polis*, the city. However, replacing individuals with corporations in these theories might prove useful – for example, why would, say, the conglomerates ran by the

---

[5] OpenSecrets.org, "Corporate Contributions to Outside Groups."
[6] Ungureanu, Mihai, Alexandru Volacu and Andra Roescu. Alegere rationala si comportament electoral (Bucharest: Tritonic-IPP, 2015).

Koch brothers invest hundreds of millions of dollars in a candidate that had no chance of winning? Why would other companies assume liberal values and promote them politically, often accompanying their vows with hefty campaign contributions to Democratic and progressive candidates? The answer is – to attract a consumer base that is simultaneously a voter base and to further their interests as companies. By this method one can make Public Choice theory more rational, adding the economic interest dimension that is prevalent in corporatist behavior. Indeed, the fatal flaw of rational choice is that individuals – obviously – do not act rationally, often going and even voting against their own interests. Companies, on the other hand, do not – if they do, the corrective mechanisms of the market steer them back onto the right path by lowering profits.

An extended involvement of corporations at a political level will have revolutionary implications in the literature, but also in day-to-day life. The consumption of undistinguishable products will be guided by the commonality of values. Consumer A will choose product B because corporation C, as opposed to corporation D, is favorable to same-sex marriage, for example. As issues will divide society, so will they divide the consumer base, creating space for corporations to emerge – just as a party comes to service an unattended part of the electorate – or forcing all corporations to meet in a moderate middle, as agreement sets over all groups. As same-sex marriage becomes widely accepted, for example, no corporation will, like Barilla, ever profess a preference for heterosexual couples. Other issues, in turn, will take to the fore of debate.

For Plattner, the tension between individual rights and majority rule within liberal democracy is clear. He states that "in recent decades, "pluralism" has increasingly been used to refer not so much to economic interests as to ethnic, cultural or religious groups, usually in a fashion that advocated wide latitude for such minorities to be able to pursue their own specific traditions and ways of life."[7] This, in turn, led to a backlash of populist movements that stress the "nation" and accuse the "foreign" interests of minorities.

But companies are less vulnerable to such a backlash of values or populist rhetoric. Corporations do not exist in a vacuum, but in the market. Governed by the iron rules of costs and benefits, the market is a daily reality to every individual and corporation. For Thomas Sowell, the market economy makes it so the "capitalist," the entrepreneur, and the workers are all in the service of the

---

[7] Marc F. Plattner, "Populism, pluralism and liberal democracy," *Journal of Democracy* 21, 1 (January 2010): pp. 81-92 https://doi.org/10.1353/jod.0.0154.

consumer, while being consumers themselves.[8] Thus, they fulfill John Stuart Mill's criterion of a legislative that should live under its own laws.[9] Moreover, they are actors that cannot thrive without existing in a plurality, the monopoly being a surefire way toward stagnation and inefficiency.

The market, unlike the existing democratic political arena and its 5, 4, 3 or 2-year cycles of elections, is a daily plebiscite on the existence and success of producers, of corporations. The company that does not abide by the wishes of the consumers – expressed immediately through their purchases or the absence thereof – will immediately face financial consequences. The same cannot be said about incumbent politicians that, once elected, can enjoy a much greater leniency from the forgetful voters with regard to their actions.

Aside from the advantages brought to internal politics, corporations may also serve as better agents in international debates, due to their current approach to international trade. As Sowell notes, "international trade is not a zero-sum game. Otherwise, nations would not continuously engage in it." Already used to plurality within the internal and international market, the majoritarian-populist-monopolist tendencies among corporations are greatly reduced. One can conclude that while corporations do a better job of promoting their own interests in front of elected officials, they are simultaneously less likely to fall prey to populism or to give in to baser instincts like stressing one's own ethnic group and its superiority. Corporations have no ethnicity, no gender, no nationality, no sexual preference, no religious identity and so on. They are vessels in which consumers pour their own values, almost unwittingly. Unlike politicians, corporations are what the consumers make of them – and they are equipped with far more powerful voices and far more workable tools of tempering.

The present chapter has shown that corporations, indeed entire industries, can be colored politically. If companies in energy largely *spoke* – donated – for Republicans, most companies in communication electronics backed Democrats, with both parties disputing the most important donor industries. This ideological diversity among corporations shows that they can spend their money to actors of both political leanings. The following chapter, however, takes progressive corporations as the main objects of study and presents 16 case studies showing how corporations exhibited values, took stances and performed actions that have until now been reserved for politicians or voters.

---

[8] Sowell, *Basic* Economics, 9-10.
[9] John Stuart Mill, *Considerations on Representative Government* (Cambridge: Cambridge University Press, 2010).

Chapter IX

Progressive Corporations

For years now, corporations have been expected to rise up to the demands of various socially-minded groups: gay rights activists, women's empowerment supporters, NGOs dedicated to the protection of the environment and various other single-issue groups. In response to these expectations, while many multinational companies pay careful attention to their policies toward minorities of all kinds, others are scolded for not keeping up the pace, not moving with the times. The Australian airliner Qantas is an example of the former. Qantas issued guidelines to its employees that taught them how to be more inclusive – by avoiding "manterrupting," saying "partner" rather than "husband," or avoiding "unconscious colonialist bias"[1] when discussing Australian history and so on. The progressive turn of Qantas was, nevertheless, heavily taxed by Australian politicians, including former Prime Minister Tony Abbott, who called the airline a "corporate thought police." The company defended itself by saying that it was simply following the suggestions given by the Diversity Council of Australia.[2] Caught between progressive activists and the possible backlash of a more conservative – yet not as active – segment of the society, corporations have had to manage a social minefield that could easily make or break a financial quarter.

The bottom line, however, is that one can no longer talk about corporations as merely profit-seeking enterprises locked in the sphere of economy. People – in their capacity of consumers – as well as some lobby groups or even state institutions, expect corporations as entities to follow specific lines that obviously fall within the political or social sphere. At the same time, they manifest a desire to keep companies politically gagged – all of these actors, conservative or progressive, are telling corporations "follow our queue, do not contribute to the public debate in any meaningful way, unless it is to agree with us."

---

[1] Moya Sarner, "Inequality at 30,000 feet: is aviation the least progressive industry?" *The Guardian*, March 6th, 2018, https://www.theguardian.com/world/shortcuts/2018/mar/06/inequality-30000-feet-qantas-aviation-least-progressive-industry.
[2] Sarner, "Inequality."

While some corporations find themselves in the deceiving political waters by mistake, and often tread wrongly in an effort to adapt, others face the challenge head-on, risking alienating some consumers in a bid to attract others. To celebrate the International Women's Day, one of the largest toy-makers in the world, Mattel, introduced a new line of its famous Barbie dolls. The 'Shero' collection paid tribute to a series of inspiring women – artists, mathematicians, filmmakers and more. In total, 16 toy Barbies were meant to inspire young girls to aim high. Mattel was not acting on its own whim, it was responding to concerns regarding the socializing effects of marketing toys by gender directly to children.[3] While critics emphasized that the image associated with the Barbie-type look – especially body-wise – has not been diminished by the move, the 'Shero' collection goes to show that even toy-makers, which one may image would normally be far away from any political debate, can come under the spotlight of the new corporate environment.[4] Promoting women has been one of the safer political stances a company could take – in 2019, only 46% of women and 61% of men in the United States declared themselves to be satisfied with how women are treated in society[5] – but it was still a gamble, as even an attempt to seem "with the times" from the part of a corporation could at best seem awkward or forced and at worst false, sparking criticism from the same activists who urge for a progressive turn.

While Mattel and other corporations chose to respond to wider societal issues, some were not afraid to tackle specific and current political topics. In June of 2018, another major scandal prompted the response of a group of corporations with regard to the policy enforced by the United States government in connection to illegal migration – the separation of migrant children from their families. American Airlines, United Airlines and Frontier Airlines took a clear stance against the policy. Facing wide-ranging criticism, President Trump announced he will overturn the policy, thus prompting another airline carrier, Delta, to publicly – and with a healthy dose of irony – commend his decision. In their statements, all three airline companies had asked the government to not use their planes in the process of transporting migrant children after they had been separated from their parents. American

---

[3] Emma Batha, "Pink for girls: does toy marketing affect girls' career choices?" *Reuters*, April 30th, 2019, https://www.reuters.com/article/us-britain-children-marketing/pink-for-girls-does-toy-marketing-affect-girls-career-choices-idUSKCN1S52AD.

[4] Mary Louise Kelly, "Mattel introduces 17 'Shero' Barbies to celebrate international women's day," *NPR*, March 8th, 2018, https://www.npr.org/2018/03/08/592046301/mattel-introduces-shero-barbies-for-international-womens-day.

[5] Megan Brenan, "Record-Low 46% of Women Pleased with Society's Treatment," *Gallup*, January 17th, 2019, https://news.gallup.com/poll/246056/record-low-women-pleased-society-treatment.aspx.

Airlines, the company that had carried refugees for NGOs as well as the government beforehand, stated that it has "no desire to be associated with separating families, or worse, to profit from it."[6] A greedy, profit-seeking corporation that faced cutthroat competition was refusing a sure and steady income – why? Because it became obvious to AA that it was now operating in a new, socio-political market, one in which making a profit and taking a stance on a social or political issue became two sides of the same coin.

Similarly, the following stories present a plethora of well-known corporations taking stances that cannot be defined as being something other than political in their essence. They tackle sexism, racism, morality, the inclusion of sexual minorities, gun ownership, the Israel-Palestine dispute, the right to protest, environmentalism, and many more. They all involve three actors – corporations, consumers and politicians – each influencing the other and thus creating the new politico-economic global market. Each involvement of the corporations into public life is, as the next pages will show, supervised and corrected by the consumers, who make use of their economic voice – their purchases – to have an immediate vote on how the corporation behaves publicly, to a degree of involvement and active participation and mobilization that present-day democracies no longer see in the party-driven political life.

Nowadays, a revolution in politics is going largely unnoticed. Those who notice it wildly misinterpret it as a corruption of the revolving doors-type, in which the wealthy business elite employs a buddy system with political leaders. The real transformative process of the American and global political system and market system is out of the hands of the elites, as much as it is out of the hands of any average citizen. The interplay between the corporate need for profits, the activist consumer base, the saturated market and the steadily declining political participation leads to the birth of a new political player – the corporation. Behind it, however, individuals are turning their mantles of voters for those of consumers, and they, as the following cases will show, retain their decision-making powers.

1. Corporations and Women's Day

McDonald's, perhaps the most well-known fast-food brand globally, also attempted its own celebration of the International Women's Day in 2018, not unlike toy-maker Mattel. Intending to honor "the accomplishments of women everywhere," the well-known restaurants were decorated for the event, with

---

6 Jackie Wattles and Rene Marsh, "Airlines ask the government not to fly separated children on their planes," *CNN Money*, June 20th, 2018, https://money.cnn.com/2018/06/20/news/companies/american-airlines-children-detention-border-trump/index.html.

one establishment in California inverting the "M" in its logo in order to form a "W."[7] Public opinion, however, was not satisfied by the gesture and proceeded to flood social media with criticism regarding the low wages that McDonald's employees – among which many women could be found – receive. Outspoken leftwing British organization Momentum, together with union allies, went as far as branding McDonald's celebration of Women's Day as "empty McFeminism."[8] A corporation could not be progressive for one day and ask the activist consumers to look away from its other flaws, the critics said.

In Malaysia, KFC experimented with its own form of celebrating Women's Day – the fast-food restaurant converted its icon, Colonel Sanders, into Claudia Sanders, the second wife of the KFC founder.[9] Following up on the story of Claudia Sanders, however, journalists discovered that she was initially hired to help the founder's first wife, which she subsequently replaced. Wanting to join the movement for gender equality and female empowerment, corporations are coming under fire from the conservative side. At the same time, they are criticized for not behind authentic from the progressive side. The same duality will be found in many of the following examples.

To celebrate women's rights and women's history month, whiskey maker Johnny Walker also announced a limited edition featuring a change in its well-known logo – no longer Johnny Walker, but Jane Walker. Diageo Plc, the parent company of the whiskey label, thus hoped to expand its client base and to state its values at the same time, since women do not traditionally prefer whiskey, viewing it as intimidating, as Johnny Walker Vice President Stephanie Jacoby explained. In total, the limited edition featured a quarter of a million bottles, each purchase prompting the company to donate a dollar to organizations that promote women – specifically those who run for office.[10] With a swift move,

---

[7] Nadia Khomami and Jessica Gleza, "'Try Again': McDonald's women's day stunt criticized as hollow gesture," *The Guardian*, March 8th, 2018, https://www.theguardian.com/business/2018/mar/08/mcdonalds-sign-international-womens-day.

[8] Khomami and Gleza, "'Try Again': McDonald's women's day stunt criticized as hollow gesture," https://www.theguardian.com/business/2018/mar/08/mcdonalds-sign-international- womens-day.

[9] David Carrig, "KFC replaces iconic Colonel Sanders with his wife to honor International Women's Day in Malaysia," *USA Today*, March 8th, 2018, https://eu.usatoday.com/story/money/business/2018/03/08/kfc-replaces-iconic-col-sanders-international-womens-day/406308002/.

[10] Jenna Amatulli, "Johnnie Walker releases 'Jane Walker' to celebrate women's rights," *Huffington Post*, February 27th, 2018, https://www.huffpost.com/entry/johnnie-walker-releases-jane-walker-whiskey-to-celebrate-womens-rights_n_5a957944e4b0bef79e3045ba.

Diageo pushed a value in order to expand its share of the market, embracing a politically-charged message and stance in order to profit.

Awkward as they may be, attempts by the corporations to be more progressive and inclusive are noteworthy in and of themselves. They signal that the traditionally profit-seeking advents are not disconnected from the debates that rage through society – although they prefer to speak out only when a clear winner is established, as in the case of feminism, and not before.

2. Corporations and Race

Racism has been – and still is – one of the major issues not only in the American society, but also in different parts of the world. In March of 2018, beer-maker Heineken faced the uproar of the South African agora after running an ad in which a freshly opened bottle of Heineken slides past several dark-skinned people in order to reach a lightly skinned woman, the commercial ending with the tone-deaf slogan "sometimes lighter is better."[11] Outraged consumers took to Twitter to express rage and to call for boycotts of Heineken beer.

Racially insensitive commercials being criticized on social media and leading to a short-term decrease in overall sales is an entirely new phenomenon for corporations, and many have paid for their lessons.

In January of 2018, clothing retail giant H&M put out a commercial which featured a black child wearing a sweatshirt with the words "coolest monkey in the jungle" imprinted on the front.[12] Musicians and other public personalities immediately condemned the ad, and in South Africa the radical militant group the Economic Freedom Fighters protested and trashed H&M stores. Protests of such violence are usually reserved for when state institutions abuse their power, infringing on democratic standards, or when discriminatory policies are approved by state legislatures. For corporations to come under similar attacks due to a message perceived as political is again, an entirely novel phenomenon, signaling that their involvement in the political and social sphere – however necessary and driven by market forces – bears risks traditionally not experienced by companies.

---

[11] Boniswa Khumalo, "Heineken gets backlash for racist lighter is better ad," *ENCA*, March 31st, 2018, https://www.enca.com/life/watch-heineken-gets-backlash-for-racist-lighter-is-better-ad.

[12] Samantha West, "HandM faced backlash over its 'monkey' sweatshirt ad. It isn't the company's only controversy," *The Washington Post*, January 19th, 2018, https://www.washingtonpost.com/news/arts-and-entertainment/wp/2018/01/19/hm-faced-backlash-over-its-monkey-sweatshirt-ad-it-isnt-the-companys-only-controversy/.

A sensitive issue such as race proved especially tricky to tackle for companies and many of them were caught in the sights of activists even when they were not intentionally expressing a political message. The consumer-enforced punishment of preference was the boycott, a method of protest that is especially effective against corporations both on the short and long-term, bringing a specific issue to public attention and then hurting the balance sheet of the company subjected to the boycott. The boycott is today a much more powerful tool than it was in the days of Elizabeth Heyrick, as it is made easier by the high degree of interchangeability of products in the producer-rich globalized market. Heineken's and H&M's detractors had a wide array of beer and clothing producers to go to after deciding to take part in the boycott of the two corporations. Their consumption, as a result, was unimpaired, whereas Heineken and H&M received the full power of their convictions translated into lost revenue. Such is the power of the consumer in the socio-political market of the politically-conscious corporations – and it is a power that greatly outweighs that of the voter in a democracy.

3. Gillette and Toxic Masculinity

On the 5th of October 2017, the *New York Times* published a story regarding allegations of acts of sexual misconduct committed by Hollywood producer Harvey Weinstein. In the following months and even years, more and more stories about powerful men using their position in order to obtain sexual favors came to light, igniting a conversation about sexism and power across the globe, especially in North America and much of Europe. The powerful social movement #MeToo left sizable marks on numerous industries and corporations have had to respond as well, as the new social actors of the globe.

Against this background, razor-maker Gillette released an ad tackling "toxic masculinity," condemning the sexual harassment and bullying that go unpunished due to an antiquated and misguided standard of what it means to be a man – a standard of masculinity kept and fostered within the collective imagination of society. The company turned its old slogan into a question, asking "is this the best a man can get?" and answering "we believe in the best in men. To say the right thing, act the right way," the words hovering over images of men defending others from bullying or harassment. In the same ad, Gillette assumes a moral responsibility in setting an example for the coming generations of men – incidentally, future customers – and embraces recent research showing that gender roles may have a harmful effect in the modern society.

"Brands like ours play a role in influencing culture,"[13] Gillette further says in a statement, making explicit the new reality. Aside from releasing its ad, the company also pledged to donate a million dollars on a yearly basis to nonprofit organizations tackling issues such as stereotypes and expectations tied to gender. At the same time, the Gillette ad, released at the beginning of 2019, *does not feature a single razor* – despite being a commercial for a company that makes razors. In a way that is revealing of the new realities of the global market, the corporation in question was selling its products not by highlighting their advantages – seeing as Gillette razors can be said to have virtually become interchangeable in terms of price and quality with razors made by competitors – but by stressing company values. This so-called "commodity activism" is thought of by marketing companies to be the new way through which large brands set out to communicate with their potential customers. In this way, a razor-making company manages to advertise its razors without actually referencing them, because *in the new market it does not matter what you sell*, but what your values are.

However, commodity activism should not be seen as a neutral concept with no larger implications for the corporation or for the society at large. Professing a series of values signals identity and, most of all, membership. Gillette, through its ad, took part in a contentious social debate and *chose a side* – the progressive side.

What was the outcome? Gillette's ad regarding toxic masculinity was released while the company was seeing a downfall in market share – from 70% of young people in 2016 to 54% in 2019.[14] With this drop in sales in the background, Gillette's marketing and executive team decided to take the brand's famous tagline – part of its identity – and bring it to the younger consumers in an altered, modern interpretation. Moreover, the company unwrapped its new identity by using the attention surrounding a public controversy. The same recipe has been followed – with somewhat less success – by Pepsi, in April of 2017, when it appeared to be portraying its soda as a pathway to social peace, all in the context of the Black Lives Matter protests.[15]

---

[13] Avery Anapol, "Gillette takes on toxic masculinity in new ad campaign," *The Hill*, January 14th, 2019, https://thehill.com/blogs/blog-briefing-room/news/425190-gillette-takes-on-toxic-masculinity-in-new-ad-campaign.

[14] Ben Kesslen, "Gillette is woke now? When brands try to keep up with the times," *Euronews*, January 15th, 2019, https://www.euronews.com/2019/01/15/gillette-woke-now-when-brands-try-keep-times-n958996.

[15] Daniel Victor, "Pepsi Pulls Ad Accused of Trivializing Black Lives Matter," *The New York Times*, April 5th, 2017, https://www.nytimes.com/2017/04/05/business/kendall-jenner-pepsi-ad.html.

Finally, the Gillette ad sparked immediate reactions from both supporters and critics. The former dubbed it a step forward toward dealing with an important issue plaguing society, while the latter issued condemnations of the ad and vowed to never buy Gillette products again. The economic boycott was again the primary method through which opponents of the ad set out to make their voices heard. These opponents, like the NGO *Citizens United* before them, decided to *speak through their money* – this time it was not contributions, but their purchases, in order to voice their concerns.

One can presuppose that a large brand makes cold calculations when it decides to market its products by connecting its image to a major social issue – it consciously accepts the very real possibility of losing some customers in order to ensure the loyalty of others. Gillette and other "progressive corporations" may have well made the right call in deciding to lead the charge – studies show that the overwhelming majority of millennials – 91%, according to one study[16] – in the United States would switch to the products of another brand *if they associate it with a cause worthy of support.*

4. Corporations and Morality

Corporations, rather than elected representatives and legislators, have also been sought after as the guardians of morality. In March of 2018, Wal-Mart pulled the Cosmopolitan magazine from its checkout aisles across the United States. The removal was the result of years of lobbying from the part of The National Center on Sexual Exploitation, a nonprofit opposed to "sexualized" content in magazines and media. In order to protect young girls and to combat pornography, the group has a history of appealing to Wal-Mart, as well as other major retailers, to remove magazines such as Cosmopolitan, which markets itself to a segment of "fearless females" from its racks. Success came only in the aftermath of the #MeToo movement, even if the movement itself set to empower women and to combat misogyny, and not to promote religiously inspired morality in a supermarket. While the magazine remained available inside the store, being removed only from the checkouts, Wal-Mart saw a variety of responses to its move. Conservatives applauded the removal, deeming it a victory. At the same time, some progressives accused the retailer of distorting the MeToo movement and, naturally, threatened to boycott. Hearst, the publisher of Cosmopolitan and other fashion magazines,

---

[16] "2015 Cone Communications Millennial CSR Study," ConeComm, accessed February 17th, 2019, https://www.conecomm.com/research-blog/2015-cone-communications-millennial-csr-study.

responded with a sentence – "To quote our Lord Jesus Christ, well done, good and faithful servant."[17]

Christianity is not the only religion which has held corporations to its rules of morality. In Iran, a country barren of secularism, liberalism and democracy, where individuals have little room for expressing discontent, boycotts are still the preferred tool of the common people, of consumers, when faced with a social issue. In June of 2019, a woman who refused to wear the hijab, the Islamic headscarf, was dropped by her taxi driver in the middle of a street in Tehran. Enraged, the woman posted a picture of the driver on social media, prompting a wave of fury against the taxi app Snapp which employed the driver.[18]

The taxi company apologized and vowed to punish Saeed Abed, the driver, for upholding Islamic values and rules not in the United Kingdom or the United States, but in Iran. Foreseeably, more conservative consumers, not unlike their counterparts in the US, started criticizing the app for giving in to the initial threats, starting their own hashtag – #boycottSnapp. As these events took place in Iran, the story did not stop there. Interviewed by a state TV channel, the taxi driver referred to his religious, but also law-bound duty, as drivers whose passengers are not wearing hijabs can be fined under Iranian law. The Islamic Revolutionary Guards, whose role is to prevent foreign interference in the Iranian system, got involved as well, taking the side of the driver and ensuring his continuing employment. Not much later, the woman who ignited the scandal apologized to the driver and the company, vowing to "comply with my country's laws."[19]

Caught between progressives and conservatives, corporations can openly choose a side, like Gillette, remain neutral and try to appease both sides in a bid to attract the *median consumer* – who is very similar to the *median voter* – like Wal-Mart or periodically shift from one stance to complete silence. At the same time, they do not respond to each of the enormous number of debates that can be found within society at any given time. Wal-Mart chose to respond to the lobbying from The National Center on Sexual Exploitation and to ban gun sales

---

[17] Amy B. Wang, "Wal-Mart pulls Cosmopolitan from checkout aisles after pressure from anti-porn group," *The Washington Post*, March 28th, 2018, https://www.washingtonpost.com/news/business/wp/2018/03/28/walmart-pulls-cosmopolitan-from-checkout-aisles-after-pressure-from-anti-porn-group/.
[18] "Iranian hardliners threaten taxi app boycott in hijab row," *BBC News*, June 11th, 2019, https://www.bbc.com/news/blogs-trending-48593981.
[19] "Iranian hardliners threaten taxi app boycott in hijab row," *BBC News*.

to anyone under 21 after the terrible school shooting in Parkland Florida[20] – but did not address issues such as race, police brutality, immigration and many others. In Iran, consumers felt a fragment of their power before they were readily pushed back by the state institutions of an oppressive regime founded on a fundamentalist interpretation of religion that is contrary to liberty.

Further research is required to determine why companies identify with some issues but not with others. The novelty of the socio-economic market that now involves corporations as primary movers and shakers, as well as the old mentality of viewing companies purely as economic advents, still prevent such vital research from being conducted. However, an educated guess would be that companies choose topics to which their consumers are most likely to respond and which they can visibly influence or in which they are already involved. One example would be Patagonia, who promotes environmental protection and sells outdoor gear.[21]

5. Barilla and LGBTQ inclusion

When they do become involved in the socio-political marketplace, corporations do not set their own identity – it is given to them by the consumers, clients who lean a certain way. If the corporation does not obey the wishes of its clients, much like an elected official who goes against the desires of his or her voters, it is readily and quickly punished.

At one point, one such corporation was Barilla, famous for being the world's largest pasta manufacturer. In 2013, the chairman of Barilla said that his company will not show ads featuring same-sex couples and that if they did not like his policy, homosexual couples could go to the competitors. The backlash was monumental – particularly in the United States, where Harvard University dumped Barilla products and gay rights activists went beyond boycotting and *started promoting other brands.*

The transformation of Barilla was incredible. In less than a year, the company based in Parma, Italy, had expanded health benefits for transgender employees and started contributing money to gay rights organizations, as well as posting

---

[20] Nathan Bomey, "Wal-Mart bans gun sales to anyone under 21 after Parkland, Florida school shooting," *USA Today*, March 1st, 2018, https://eu.usatoday.com/story/money/2018/02/28/walmart-bans-gun-sales-anyone-under-21-after-parkland-florida-school-shooting/383487002/.

[21] "Environmental and Social Responsibility," Patagonia, accessed December 3rd, 2019, https://www.patagonia.com/environmentalism.html.

an ad showing a lesbian couple on its website.[22] Barilla was soon rewarded by gay rights watchdogs that take gay-friendliness as a measure to rate companies and subsequently, their products. Guido Barilla, chairman of Barilla, therefore issued numerous apologies between 2013 and 2014, seeking to temper the wave of criticism within a market that is now not only financial, but also deeply political. The same Barilla, through its Foundation, is now in its 10th year of organizing the International Forum on Food and Nutrition, seeking to encourage governments, fellow corporations and NGOs to cut back on the CO2 emissions caused by food production, to make people's diets sustainable for the environment.[23]

6. Chick-fil-A and Christianity

Other companies underwent the same transformative treatment as Barilla. In 2010 and 2012 respectively, Target and Chick-fil-A came under fire for supporting anti-gay candidates and were subjected to boycotts. Amazingly, conservative groups actually started a movement of support toward Chick-fil-A for the same reason, revealing the possibility of classifying fast-food diners as "progressive" and "conservative." In the new reality, progressive consumers were going out of their way to avoid Chick-fil-A while conservative ones bought the products of the same fast-food restaurant – both doing so in order to *express their values through their money, their purchases.*

The restaurant's identity followed it abroad as well. In fact, Chick-fil-A's reputation as a conservative corporation opposed to same-sex marriage[24] meant that the opening of its first restaurant in the UK was met with protests. Opening in Reading, the Atlanta-based fast-food chain was received by the LGBTQ advocacy group Reading Pride, who urged locals to boycott the restaurant and convinced a mall to refrain from prolonging the restaurant's lease. On social media, pro-LGBT activists on social media used the hashtag #GetTheChickOut to show their opposition to Chick-fil-A. The protests were so effective that after six months in the United Kingdom, the chain announced

---

[22] Sandhya Somashekhar, "Human Rights campaign says Barilla has turned around its policies on LGBT," *The Washington Post*, November 19th, 2014, https://www.wa shingtonpost.com/politics/human-rights-campaign-says-barilla-has-turned-around -its-policies-on-lgbt/2014/11/18/9866efde-6e92-11e4-8808-afaa1e3a33ef_story.html.
[23] Euronews, "Barilla, the company that is trying to tackle the climate crisis," December 9th, 2019, https://www.euronews.com/2019/12/07/barilla-the-company-that-is-trying-to-tackle-the-climate-crisis.
[24] K. Allan Blume, "'Guilty as charged,' Cathy says of Chick-fil-A's stand on biblical and family values," *Baptist Press*, July 16th, 2012, http://www.bpnews.net/38271/guilty-as-charged-cathy-says-of-chickfilas-stand-on-biblical-and-family-values.

that it will be closing shop and leaving.[25] Starved of the American conservative support that allows it to make profits, Chick-fil-A's British adventure ended abruptly.

The same Chick-fil-A closes its restaurants in the US every Sunday – to honor God. By doing so, it obviously loses the revenue of half of the weekend crowds, well over 1 billion dollars.[26] The practice seemingly started from the founders of the chain, the devout Cathy family.[27] Right now, however, being close to God is part of Chick-fil-A's corporate identity.

Chick-fil-A's political activism and its effects will perhaps serve as a case study in the future. In November of 2019, the fast-food chain, following the same course charted by Barilla years earlier, announced that it will no longer fund The Salvation Army and the Fellowship of Christian Athletes, organizations that have historically opposed same-sex marriage.[28] Instead, the corporation's donations were to find their way to more politically neutral issues such as "hunger, homelessness and education."[29] The chain also promised to donate to any organization that tackles these issues, irrespective of the accent it puts on faith.

Aside from boycotts affecting short-term income, a corporation seeks to preserve its image through its ads and generally perceived behavior. Appearing to be ahead of times can somewhat convey that same impression about one's products – even if they are not. Catering to new markets – gay couples or liberally-minded millennial – can also be a good financial decision.

Boycotts are not new in the corporate world, as Elizabeth Heyrick's 1790 boycott of companies that used slave labor showed. In 1977, Nestle faced a 7-year long boycott from its critics and their supporters due to the company's

---

[25] Marina Pitofsky, "Chick-Fil-A closing first UK restaurant after protests," *The Hill*, October 19th, 2019, https://thehill.com/blogs/blog-briefing-room/news/466604-Chick-fil-A-closing-first-uk-restaurant-after-protests.

[26] Kate Taylor, "Chick-fil-A likely loses out on more than $1 billion in sales every year by closing on Sundays — and it's a brilliant business strategy," *Business Insider*, July 29th, 2019, https://www.businessinsider.com/Chick-fil-A-closes-on-sunday-why-2019-7.

[27] Taylor, "Chick-fil-A."

[28]Catherine Thorbecke, "Chick-fil-A will no longer fund organizations with anti-LGBTQ ties," *ABC News*, November 19th, 2019, https://abcnews.go.com/Business/chick-fil-longer-fund-anti-lgbtq-organizations/story?id=67111125.

[29] "Chick-fil-A Foundation announces 2020 priorities to address education, homelessness and education," TheChickenWire, November 18th, 2019, https://thechickenwire.Chick-fil-A.com/news/Chick-fil-A-foundation-announces-2020-priorities.

practice of marketing breast milk substitutes in developing countries.[30] By 1982, however, Nestle became the first manufacturer to develop and apply a marketing code inspired by the World Health Organization's recommendations, resulting in the dropping of the boycott in 1984. Nowadays, Nestle prides itself with how it handled the crisis, displaying its entire history on its website.[31]

However, while these strategic boycotts of a company and its entire line of products sought to influence company policies, the boycott of a company as punishment for a political act such as financing or supporting a group through ads is new, both in scope and in purpose. The same can be said about the reverse, rewarding a company for a similar action.

7. Target, Best Buy and consumer boycotts

One case proves revealing of the new trend, which connects companies to non-economic, but social and political issues. In 2010, right after the *Citizens United* ruling by the Supreme Court, the well-known low-cost clothes retailer Target decided to donate $150,000 in campaign contributions to Tom Emmer, who back then was the Republican gubernatorial candidate for Minnesota and who opposed abortion and same-sex marriage, also taking a clear and harsh anti-immigration stance. In reply, some consumers called for a nation-wide boycott of Target stores, starting online petitions and calls directed at other consumers to boycott as well. These were not citizens gathering in protest of a government act or a bill in the Congress, nor were they mobilizing for a vote. They were individuals who discovered that within the debate regarding same-sex marriage, their voices as consumers were much stronger than those of voters or citizens.

It was a Minnesota grandmother, Randi Reitan, who became the face of the boycott movement.[32] To support her gay son, the woman filmed herself cutting her Target credit card. The video, familiar in the age of burning Nike shoes to show opposition to its ad featuring Colin Kaepernick, became instantly viral in 2010. Randi Reitan was by no means wealthy, and her decision to actively boycott a company to whom she had been a faithful customer – as her Target

---

[30] Jerry Davis, "Why the NRA boycott has been so successful so quickly," *Business Insider*, March 3rd, 2018, https://www.businessinsider.com/why-nra-boycott-so-successful-so-quickly-2018-3.

[31] "Why was a Nestle boycott launched?" *Nestle*, https://www.nestle.com/ask-nestle/our-company/answers/nestle-boycott.

[32] David Gura, "Mad about corporate donations, customers boycott Target, Best Buy," *NPR*, August 4th, 2010, https://www.npr.org/sections/thetwo-way/2010/08/04/128974389/mad-about-corporate-political-donations-customers-boycott-target-best-buy.

credit card showed – demonstrates the intensity with which people can stand by their values.

To defend itself, the corporation argued that it had made the donation to "an independent expenditure campaign – not approved by any candidate" which only later decided to throw its weight behind Emmer. In a statement released by Target's CEO, the company also reconfirmed its commitment to diversity and inclusion of members of the community of sexual minorities, citing its high rating with the Human Rights Campaign Corporate Equality Index.

Another corporation that, back in 2010, donated to MN Forward – the organization which then moved to support Emmer – was Best Buy. The retailer, long seen as an ally of the progressive agenda, gave another $100,000 in contributions to the conservative candidate, sparking the anger of liberal consumers. OutFront Minnesota, a gay rights group, immediately denounced the betrayal of a company that was supposed to be liberal.[33]

The power of corporate speech cannot be denied. After North Carolina passed its "bathroom bill" in 2016, requiring transgender people in state-run buildings to use the bathrooms corresponding to the sex on their birth certificates, corporations and other associations started to boycott the state altogether in order to not be associated with an endorsement of the bill. PayPal went back on plans to build a facility in the state, NBA moved its All-Star Game out of Charlotte and the TV production company Lionsgate decided to not go on with its activity in the same city. CoStar, Voxpro, Deutsche Bank and Adidas decided to open new facilities in other areas as well, prompting Bank of America CEO Brian Moynihan to tell CNBC that "companies are moving to other places because they don't face an issue that they face here."[34] After three years of boycotts and pressure in courts, North Carolina replaced the "bathroom bill" with another, House Bill 142, which gave the state legislature power to regulate bathroom access without subsequent definitions.[35]

In Europe as well as the U.S., corporations have chosen to position themselves on same-sex marriage and gay rights. In Hungary, the governmental Consumer Protection Department of Pest County fined Coca-

[33] Brian Montopoli, "Target boycott movement grows following donation to support 'antigay' candidate," *CBS News*, July 28th, 2010, https://www.cbsnews.com/news/target-boycott-movement-grows-following-donation-to-support-antigay-candidate/.
[34] "'Bathroom bill' to cost North Carolina $3.76 billion," *CNBC News*, March 27th, 2017, https://www.cnbc.com/2017/03/27/bathroom-bill-to-cost-north-carolina-376-billion.html.
[35] Alex Dobuzinskis, "North Carolina 'bathroom bill' settlement approved," *Reuters*, July 23rd, 2019, https://www.reuters.com/article/us-north-carolina-lgbt/north-carolina-bathroom-bill-settlement-approved-idUSKCN1UI2IJ.

Cola for featuring same-sex couples in its ads. The ad was accompanied by a campaign with posters and the #loveislove tag. The Hungarian authorities motivated the fine by saying that the Coca-Cola campaign damaged the emotional and moral development of children and minors.

In reply, Coca-Cola, one of the most recognizable brands in the world and a corporate giant valued at $81 billion worldwide – the GDP of Hungary in 2017 was $139 billion[36] – and directly employing 1,100 people in Hungary, creating 13,000 additional jobs[37] through its supply chain, said that "we are all equal, regardless of nationality, religion, gender, age, ethnicity, spoken language, hobbies, and opinions" and both heterosexuals and homosexuals have the right to love the person they choose the way it is best for them."[38] Calls for boycotting Coca-Cola surfaced immediately, led by Istvan Boldog, a conservative member of the Hungarian parliament. Others, such as the Háttér gay rights group, however, welcomed the corporation's statement.[39]

What was the context? Hungary, along with Poland, has been becoming increasingly conservative under the leadership of PM Viktor Orban and his ruling right-wing FIDESZ party. In February of 2019, to mark his opposition to immigration from the Middle East into Europe, Orban vowed to protect 'Christian Europe'[40] against all threats – and that includes progressive corporations such as Coca-Cola.

Just like parties and politicians, corporations nowadays have values, assumed stances and a base of supporters – the faithful consumers. It would not be wrong to compare, then, a contribution made by the supposedly liberal Best Buy to a conservative campaign to the defection of a Democratic senator to the Republican caucus. Both cases leave supporters disappointed and values crossed, even if for different reasons and with different intentions. Corporations, at present, are representatives of their consumers, who in turn

---

[36] "World Development Indicators," World Bank, accessed December 8th 2019, http://datatopics.worldbank.org/world-development-indicators/.

[37] "Our impact in numbers," Coca-Cola HBC Magyarorszag, accessed December 12th, 2019, https://hu.coca-colahellenic.com/en/local-impact/our-impact-in-numbers/.

[38] Fanni Kaszas, "Coca-Cola Fined for Ads with Same-Sex Couples 'Undermining Adolescents' Moral Development'," *Hungary Today*, October 15th, 2019, https://hungary today.hu/coca-cola-fined-for-ads-with-same-sex-couples-undermining-adolescents-mor al-development/.

[39] "Pro-LGBT Coca-Cola adverts spark boycott calls in Hungary," *The Guardian*, August 5th, 2019, https://www.theguardian.com/world/2019/aug/05/pro-lgbt-coca-cola-ads-spark-boy cott-calls-in-hungary.

[40] "Hungary's Orban vows defence of 'Christian' Europe," *France24*, February 10th, 2019, https://www.france24.com/en/20190210-hungarys-orban-vows-defence-christian-eur ope.

identify with them, just like Randi Reitan identified with Target before it went against her values.

8. Corporations and gun-ownership

As an organization counting five million members, the National Rifle Association has been able to exert massive pressure on elected officials and corporations alike. While the former passed legislation favoring gun-owners and stood for their values, the latter offered them advantageous deals and discounts on their products. In this way, the NRA worked as a caucus, an organized group of voters able to pressure politicians, and as an equally disciplined community of consumers courted by corporations, skillfully playing the intertwining political and market system and showcasing the synthesis of the two.

After the February 14th 2018 shooting at Marjory Stoneman Douglas high school, however, everything changed by 180 degrees – but following the same logic. This time the corporations started responding to a wider base of active and organized consumers, just like parties would to a majority of the voters.[41] Safely covered by long mandates, the U.S. Congress and Senate made no major change regarding gun policies in the country, disregarding the storm of legitimate complaints which touched upon safety and the right of children to study without the threat of bullets. Corporations had no such protections, and had to respond.

Initially, corporations wooed the NRA and its membership base in order to get ahead of their competitors. To be seen as pro-gun was to attract the loyalty and business of millions, while neutrality to the issue was punished by a smaller yet active base of gun-owners. The general public did not care much – despite previous shootings – as owning a gun can by now be considered part of the American culture. After the shooting, however, corporations rushed to sever their connections with gun enthusiasts in order to prevent alienating those that supported the anti-gun students-turned-advocates and their allies – who vastly outnumbered the NRA and who knew exactly where to apply pressure.

As a result, a week after the shooting, the First National Bank of Omaha stopped using credit cards issued with the NRA sigil on them, arguing that it had received feedback on the topic from its customers. Lockton and Chubb, the backers of the insurance policies designed for NRA members to cover their legal costs in case of a shooting, followed suit, cancelling all standing connections

---

[41] "American companies snub the National Rifle Association," *The Economist*, March 1st, 2018, https://www.economist.com/business/2018/03/01/american-companies-snub-the-national-rifle-association.

with the group. Even if Chubb had decided on the move months prior to the tragedy, the company decided to publicize the decision for the same reason as all the other corporations. Stepping away from the NRA was deemed essential by corporations wishing to preserve the mainstream base of consumers, who were horrified by the Stoneman Douglas shooting and were beginning to realize – again – the incredibly easy access that Americans have to rifles and guns.

On the other side, conservatives and NRA members organized boycotts of their own, targeting every company that had turned its back on them. Standing by their values despite the shooting, conservatives proposed their own solution to the problem – which invariably involved providing more people with guns.

Caught between a progressive rock and a conservative hard place, the corporate world is forced to take sides based on projected returns. Those that did not were not spared – the delivery company FedEx, the retailer Amazon and tech giant Apple continued to do business with the NRA, gathering cries in support of a boycott from the liberal side.

The NRA episode proves instructive as to the theoretical gap within political science literature with regard to corporate political identity and involvement. The traditional left-right ideological division was formed and is still generally upheld in relation to the involvement of the state in private affairs, be they economic or social. No such debates or theories exist yet for corporations and their measure of involvement in the political debates of the age. In the aftermath of the Stoneman Douglas shooting, commentators and public personalities – some from the left, a fact which surely made every leftwing theorist that came before them swirl around in their respective coffins – suggested that banks could block transactions for assault weapons even if they are allowed by the federal government. Simply put, a corporation – a bank, no less – should have the power, according to such a proposal, to legally block a purchase of an available, legal product from the free market made by a supposedly rational, free individual, because that product can be used in anti-social ways. Banks, in this way, should become regulators of what an individual can and should do, irrespective of the existing laws of the land. Proponents of such a measure correctly identified that banks and corporations in general make possible, through their handling of goods and finances, certain rights like the one to own a gun. At the same time, they can also block it. "In the area of processes of political corporations," as Crane et al. note, "the corporate role is actually rather more indirect. Corporations might help to facilitate, enable, or block certain political processes in society, rather than directly taking over formerly governmental prerogatives."[42]

To answer all these adversities and corporate betrayals, the NRA argued that its detractors will be replaced by their competitors.[43] Inevitably, their supporters, as well as other conservatives, will move to purchase their goods of choice from companies that share their views – even if out of purely financial reasons. Thus, the polarization of the political sphere will spread to the market, marking down some companies as progressive and others as conservative.

The aftermath of the Stoneman Douglas shooting proved revealing of the new socio-economic market in which corporations are crucial players, acting as citizens before the state and as representatives before their consumer base. The nexus between politics and business is so strong that many people living today in democracies – from the United States to India – take it for granted. In Georgia, state lawmakers went as far as defending the National Rifle Association, the group funded through individual subscriptions of supporters but also by the largest gun-makers in America, from other corporations. Delta Air Lines, the carrier that had previously agreed to discount deals with the NRA for the association's members, announced that it will be ending its ties with the pro-gun group in the wake of the Stoneman Douglas High School shooting. As a response, Casey Cagle, the Lieutenant governor of Georgia, a Republican, stated that he will "kill any tax legislation that benefits Delta unless the company changes its position and fully reinstates its relationship with the NRA."[44] In this way, the debate came full circle when it came to guns, touching consumers, corporations and only through them the state.

What was happening in Georgia, in effect, was that a democratically-elected representative, a state official, was exercising his mandate of representing the gun-owners that lived in his state and who voted for him, in front of a corporation, which was representing an anti-gun vein that had opened in the wake of the Stoneman Douglas Shooting. Both were representing interests – one of the voters, the other of consumers. However, Delta, in expressing its rejection for the NRA and its members, was responding to more recent claims.

[42] Andrew Crane, Dirk Matten and Jeremy Moon, *Corporations and Citizenship* (Cambridge: Cambridge University Press, 2008), 66.
[43] "American companies snub the National Rifle Association," *The Economist*, March 1st, 2018, https://www.economist.com/business/2018/03/01/american-companies-snub-the-national-rifle-association.
[44] Amber Phillips, "Georgia Republicans are crossing an ethically murky line by threatening Delta over its NRA boycott," *The Washington Post*, February 27th, 2018, https://www.washingtonpost.com/news/the-fix/wp/2018/02/27/georgia-republicans-are-crossing-an-ethically-murky-line-by-threatening-delta-over-its-nra-boycott/.

Had it not done so, it would have faced immediate repercussions from consumers who would have chosen different airlines that were closer to their anti-gun values. The Lieutenant governor of Georgia, on the other hand, was safe from any immediate backlash due to his years-long mandate. The Georgia episode reveals how corporations can act as representatives of their consumers, and how they are forced to do so immediately, being more reactive and responsive to complaints than politicians and representatives. A corporation lives off of its consumers *on an everyday basis* – and consuming, purchasing, is something that everyone necessarily does. A politician, on the other hand, can at times go against the wishes of a majority of those that he or she represents because elections take place in long cycles, and the public memory is short, even shorter than the percentages of people who vote. As a result, Casey Cagle could take the widely-criticized stance of defending the NRA even after a horrendous public shooting. Delta, on the other hand, could not.

But the story does not end there. The playing field is not even for both politicians and the recently-political corporations, and a keen eye has to be kept on customers, employees and other companies. The Georgia governor that threatened Delta, for example, perhaps ended any chance that the city of Atlanta had of housing the second headquarters of Amazon, whose owner, Jeff Bezos, also finances the liberal *Washington Post*, and has been repeatedly attacked by the President. Showing oneself to be opposed to the values governing a liberal corporation can drive away all likeminded companies, a serious risk for any community in need of investment. Wanting a "stable and business-friendly environment,"[45] Amazon and its 25,000 jobs chose to go to Crystal City, Virginia, due to its educated workforce and commitment to technology. Moreover, the corporation received a warm welcome in Crystal City.[46]

Across the pond as well, corporations were having run-ins with politicians. In May of 2019, Brexit party founder and leader Nigel Farage was campaigning in Newcastle upon Tyne when a young man flung a milkshake at him, covering him in its contents. A debate regarding political speech and violence ensued in the United Kingdom, with the projectile-milkshake attracting some people who wished to express their political views. Two subsequent milkshakes hit

[45] Abha Bhattarai, "Amazon is seeking a home for HQ2, a $5 billion second headquarters somewhere in North America," *The Washington Post*, September 8th, 2017, https://www.washingtonpost.com/news/business/wp/2017/09/07/amazon-is-looking-for-a-city-to-site-a-second-5-billion-headquarters/.
[46] Scott Cohn, "Amazon reveals the truth on why it nixed NY and chose Virginia for HQ2," *CNBC*, July 10th, 2019, https://www.cnbc.com/2019/07/10/amazon-reveals-the-truth-on-why-it-nixed-ny-and-chose-virginia-for-hq2.html.

anti-Islam, far-right leader Tommy Robison, but finally the original milkshake-thrower was given a 12-month Community Order, 150 hours of unpaid work and had to pay Farage compensation for his damaged suit.[47]

As part of the debate, however, corporations also their role. First up was McDonald's, who decided, at the request of the police, to stop selling ice creams and milkshakes in Edinburgh while Nigel Farage held a rally there. A member of the Scottish Socialist Party photographed the sign outside of the McDonald's in Edinburgh which informed customers that the venue was not serving the particular foods and posted it on Twitter, where it soon became trending.[48]

Noticing the viral picture and aware of the debates, Burger King chose to remind its customers in Scotland that it was "selling milkshakes all weekend,"[49] ending with a mischievous "have fun." In this way, the fast-food chain was seemingly just marketing its products – except that one of them, the milkshake, had been politicized by the past events, and Burger King was subtly marking its support. Soon thereafter, Burger King was accused of no less than inciting violence – politically-motivated violence. Social media was flooded by supporters of Brexit criticizing the chain's previous message.

9. Corporations and the Parkland Shooting

While the Parkland shooting ignited debates regarding the NRA and gun-ownership in general, it also caused politically-minded messages to spark up from unexpected places. Nickelodeon, the broadcaster specialized in TV shows for children, for example, also took a public stance. On March 14th, the survivors turned anti-gun lobbyists of Parkland staged a national walkout to protest existing gun laws in the United States. On the same day, Nickelodeon paused its usual program for 17 minutes – to honor the 17 students and faculty members that were killed – and issued a simple message of support of the walkout.[50] Social media users were again divided by the broadcaster's action,

---

[47] Martin Evans, "Man who attacked Nigel Farage with milkshake is ordered to pay cleaning bill after admitting assault charge," *Telegraph*, June 18th, 2019, https://www.telegraph.co.uk/news/2019/06/18/man-attacked-nigel-farage-milkshake-admits-assault-charge/.

[48] Joe Roberts, "Burger King accused of 'inciting violence' against Farage by selling milkshakes," *MetroNews*, May 19th, 2019, https://metro.co.uk/2019/05/19/burger-king-accused-inciting-violence-farage-selling-milkshakes-9598586/.

[49] Roberts, "Burger King accused of 'inciting violence' against Farage by selling milkshakes," https://metro.co.uk/2019/05/19/burger-king-accused-inciting-violence-farage-selling-milkshakes-9598586/.

[50] Cortney Roark, "Nickelodeon went off the air for 17 minutes at the time of the national walkout," *USA Today*, March 14th, 2018, https://eu.usatoday.com/story/life/nation-now/2018/03/14/nickelodeon-went-off-air-17-minutes-national-walkout/424430002/.

with liberals expressing their utter support, while the conservatives did the exact opposite.

Even when a corporation may want to appear progressive, socially responsible and forward-thinking, the conservative backlash comes as punishment. The Parkland shooting received international attention and spawned strong anti-gun movements that sought to pressure both elected representatives and profit-seeking and traditionally apolitical corporations. After Dick's Sporting Goods decided to stop selling guns to anyone under 21 years old, although the laws of the state of Michigan say that 18 is old enough to purchase firearms, an 18-year old filed a suit against the company. The young man claimed to be discriminated under Michigan law on the basis of his age. Earlier the same year, another man filed a similar report against the retailer Wal-Mart for the same reason.[51]

In media as well as in politics, corporations are acquiring a stronger voice – and people, from their positions of consumers as well as voters, are welcoming it. After Fox News's Laura Ingraham, star of "The Ingraham Angle," mocked David Hogg, a survivor of the Parkland school shooting, eleven major companies decided to stop advertising on her show.

What had happened was that in the aftermath of the shooting, Hogg became a well-known activist for gun control, alongside many of his classmates. Rejected by four colleges during his senior year, Hogg was mocked by the conservative Ingraham, prompting his call for a boycott of her show, asking his more than half a million social media followers to contact big companies and ask them to renounce Ingraham.[52] The results did not delay. TripAdvisor, Wayfair, Nestle, Johnson & Johnson, Expedia and other corporations answered the call, deciding to pull their ads from Ingraham's show, which was removed from TV streaming platforms as well. 24 hours after Hogg issued his appeal to companies through their customers, Ingraham, an early supporter of Donald Trump and a longtime right-wing media personality, apologized. The corporations had spoken – acting as representatives of their liberal base – and their voice was stronger than that of "natural" persons. Hogg and his supporters found a stronger avatar in the person of the "artificial" persons of Johnson &

---

[51] Morgan Gstalter, "Michigan 18-year-old sues Dick's over new gun age rule," *The Hill*, March 9th, 2018, https://thehill.com/blogs/blog-briefing-room/news/377597-michigan-18-year-old-sues-dicks-over-new-gun-age-rule.
[52] Brad Tuttle, "All the advertisers dropping Laura Ingraham after she mocked Parkland survivor David Hogg," *Time*, March 30th, 2018, https://money.com/laura-ingraham-david-hogg-advertising-boycott/.

Johnson, Nestle and others. Their complaints were heard only when they were conveyed by the stronger voice of the companies.

Critics of the *Citizens United* ruling say that it gives corporations a political weight that cannot be matched by the citizens. But in the Laura Ingraham case, it was the citizens that appealed to the corporations to act toward a political goal. While politicians could hide behind gerrymandered electoral districts and long electoral cycles, not to mention strong partisan caucuses, corporations have to respond to their consumers every day, otherwise they could be punished by their move toward a more responsive competitor.

In her article for the *Washington Post*, Bruenig calls the treatment that Ingraham underwent in her clash with Hogg and the companies a "capital strike," a moment in which "investors withdraw or withhold investments *en masse* because they have determined that potential hazards outweigh potential gains."[53] Wholly different from traditional labor strikers or even the politically-motivated marches, rallies and pressure put on various decision-making bodies, capital strikes represent the top-down measures taken by corporations seeking to protect their image. These companies, in and of themselves, may not want to impact the behavior or speech of a particular TV or radio personality, on whose show they previously advertised their products. Their goal is to reach, through marketing, an audience that is as wide as possible and thus maximize sales. It is groups of citizens such as those rallied around David Hogg or the online activist group Sleeping Giants, which lobbies companies to pull their ads and thus punish those they disagree with, that force corporations to act and take sides. Through their ads and money, corporations have become unwilling – but incredibly effective – regulators of public speech.

Boycotts, the weapon of choice for consumer-activists, are not to be disregarded. In the November 2018 Senate elections, the Republicans safely managed to defend their majority – whereas in the House, the "blue wave" made Democratic leader Nancy Pelosi Speaker of the House. In 2019, the newly elected Senate chose – in the midst of the longest government shutdown in U.S. history – as its first bill one which had as its goal the defense of the Israeli government from a boycott.

The bill, previously known as S.170 in the 2016 legislative and more recently re-introduced by Florida Senator Marco Rubio, gave state and local governments the authority to boycott any U.S. company which in turn was

---

[53] Elizabeth Bruenig, "Laura Ingraham's advertisers aren't really staging a boycott. It's a capital strike," *The Washington Post*, April 4th, 2018, https://www.washingtonpost. com/ opinions/laura-ingrahams-advertisers-arent-really-staging-a-boycott-its-a-capital-strike/ 2018/04/04/aba91dd2-382a-11e8-acd5-35eac230e514_story.html.

boycotting Israel.[54] The federal government of the United States was, in effect, instructing the states to punish companies – and individual contractors – which expressed a thoroughly political stance by banning them from working with any public institution. The federal government was doing what numerous other infuriated groups of consumers did to voice their opposition to the political stance of a corporation – it was boycotting them.

Declared unconstitutional by several federal courts due to its violation of First Amendment rights, the bill proved to be another battleground for the rights of companies. According to District Judge Diana J. Humetewa, cited by *The Intercept*, restricting the ability of companies to participate in collective calls meant to oppose Israel amounted to placing a burden on the freedom of expression of said companies.[55] It is important to note that the bill was cosponsored by several Democrats, proving that some issues were still bipartisan.

While tough regulation such as the right-to-work and anti-strike laws, in effect the deathbringers of organized labor, lay down the rules for workers' strikes, no equivalent exists for corporations and their "capital strikes." An entirely different breed of corporate acts, accepted by the companies themselves or foisted upon them by the citizens, the capital strikes will need a new kind of regulation in continuation of their recognition as persons on the basis of the *Citizens United* decision of the United States Supreme Court. Free speech rights for "artificial persons" – i.e. corporations – means an immense change to the political scene and discourse in the United States. In the new reality, corporations act as citizens, representatives and regulators.

10. Uber & Lyft and the Muslim Ban

The anti-gun public environment created by the Parkland shooting caused numerous responses from corporations big and small – either supporting or opposing the movement seeking to put into place extensive background checks or other measures that would have limited the access to guns of the general public. The same environment that pressured the backers of Ingraham's show to pull their ads also made Lyft, the on-demand transportation service, to

---

[54] S.170 was, as its subtitle clearly states, a bill meant "to provide for nonpreemption of measures by State and local governments to divest from entities that engage in commerce-related or investment-related boycott, divestment, or sanctions activities targeting Israel."

[55] Ryan Grim and Glenn Greenwald, "U.S. Senate's first bill, in the midst of shutdown, is a bipartisan defense of the Israeli government from boycotts," *The Intercept*, January 5th, 2019, https://theintercept.com/2019/01/05/u-s-senates-first-bill-in-midst-of-shutdown-is-a-bipartisan-defense-of-the-israeli-government-from-boycotts/.

announce that it will be providing free rides to students attending the anti-gun March for Our Lives rallies that occurred in late March of 2018. The move was met with cheers from the survivors of the Stoneman Douglas school shooting and with promises made by others that they will be using Lyft from that point onwards to the detriment of Uber, which remained silent on the matter.[56]

Moreover, Uber, the leading car-hailing app, also suffered from a bad record on politically-charged issues after it introduced high prices – due to high demand – to and from JFK airport during a 2017 taxi strike protesting executive order 13769, better known as the Trump administration's "Muslim ban." Back then, Uber's profit-seeking and politically-insensitive practices caused a virtual uproar, with people joining the #deleteUber movement.

In response of the same "Muslim ban," Lyft, Uber's direct competitor, went the other way and again pushed a liberal message, donating one million dollars to the American Civil Liberties Union a few hours after the tag became trending. In return, the consumers awarded the company with increased profits. Between 2017 and 2018, Lyft doubled its ride bookings and gained 40% of the market share in certain parts of the United States.[57] According to mere market logic, Uber did nothing wrong – when demand is high, prices naturally rise. When more people sought to get to the JFK airport in 2017, Uber's prices rose. Lyft, on the other hand, consciously gave up momentary revenue increases in favor of long-lasting gains in terms of reputation, ensuring consumer loyalty and prolonged growth.

The treatment received by Lyft from the part of the liberal consumers after its show of support for the anti-gun efforts vastly differed from the one experienced by the companies whose ads ran on Ingraham's talk show, which had to deal with threats of boycotting and of tremendous loss of public capital had they continued to back the conservative personality. In the new reality, the wishes and values of consumers are both the stick and the carrot that drives companies and corporations to be representatives. The same logic forces the companies to be tempered in their show of support – a radical stance assumed by a corporation would mean the total alienation of a significant part of the consumers and revenues that would be lost forever. Instead, corporations preferred a centrist position with regard to issues such as the Muslim ban and gun violence. When the public unquestionably swayed in opposition to the

---

[56] Laura Bliss, "Lyft will offer free rides to anti-gun rallies," *CityLab*, March 2nd, 2018, https://www.citylab.com/transportation/2018/03/lyft-will-offer-free-rides-to-anti-gun-rallies/554756/.

[57] Deirdre Bosa, "Lyft claims it now has more than one-third of the US ride-sharing market," *CNBC*, March 14th, 2018, https://www.cnbc.com/2018/05/14/lyft-market-share-051418-bosa-sf.html.

ban, so did the corporations. Their moderating interest, not unlike that of parties and politicians, is to appeal to the widest specter of the consumer base as possible. "Median voter" is now "median consumer."

In retrospect, dozens of corporations decided to link their names and brands with the hopeful and extremely popular anti-gun activism of the Parkland shooting survivors. Others simply cut ties with the NRA, seen as the proponent of gun ownership. These companies switched with ease from the casual relationship they had with the NRA, or the relaxed neutrality via the issue of guns, to a more activist stance, responding – in a very short amount of time – to the newly dominant values in society, unlike some elected officials. Airlines such as Delta and United, car rental companies such as Hertz and Avis and insurance providers such as MetLife renounced any connection with the conservative National Rifle Association.

11. Airbnb and the West Bank

The historically strenuous relationship between Arabs and Jews in the Middle East is perhaps the most obvious geopolitical problem in the world. Wars have been fought, treaties have been signed, negotiations have been brokered and so forth, all with the participation and arbitration of the United States, the European Union and the United Nations, often to no end, leaving a bloody and still tense stalemate to govern Israel and Palestine.

In November 2018, the rental service Airbnb decided to remove all listings in the Israeli settlements of the occupied West Bank. It did so after having been criticized for two years for listing rooms and apartments in the region by activists and even representatives of Palestine. Even though the measure did not affect too many people – about 200 houses and flats were up for booking and were subsequently taken down, and therefore the economic hit taken by Airbnb users was minimal – it offered a powerful message.

In a released statement, Airbnb noted that "the Israeli settlements in the occupied West Bank are at the core of the dispute between Israelis and Palestinians;" moreover, the company offered understanding, saying that "we know that people will disagree with this decision and appreciate their perspective. This is a controversial issue. [...] Our hope is that someday sooner rather than later, a framework is put in place where the entire global community is aligned so there will be a resolution to this historic conflict."[58]

A corporation issuing such a stance on perhaps the most controversial and unsolvable issue in one of the most volatile regions of the globe is likely to cause

---

[58] "Listings in Disputed Regions," Airbnb Press Room, November 19th, 2018, https://news.airbnb.com/listings-in-disputed-regions/.

political theorists to be taken aback. However, Palestinian activists, including Human Rights Watch, commended Airbnb for its decision and argued that Booking.com, another large online rental service for apartments and flats, should follow suit. At the same time, protest could be heard from the Israeli side.

When all is said and done, one can conclude that today, corporations are called upon to issue a coherent stance on a wide range of political and social problems – from gender debates, LGBTQ inclusion, police brutality and even the conflict between Israel and Palestine.

12. Tiffany's and Transparency

In lieu of further research, one can only posit that progressive values have had more of an impact on corporations than conservative ones in this new world. Even businesses that have been active in traditionally shady domains such as jewelry and diamonds have responded to the transformative changes of the modern global market. At the start of 2019, Tiffany's & Co., the New York-based century-old giant of the jewelry market, announced that it will bring a renewed transparency to its supply chain by revealing the source of its diamonds to each consumer. The country of origin will, therefore, be added to the information that a customer is provided with upon buying a ring or necklace at Tiffany's. The company's website stipulates that "Tiffany has a zero-tolerance policy towards conflict diamonds. We have taken vigorous steps to assure that conflict diamonds do not enter our inventory. Tiffany buys diamonds directly from the mine, where possible, and always from countries that are participants in the Kimberley Process."[59]

In this way, the company hopes that the more globally-aware and politically-minded consumer may be inclined to spend more in order to be certain that their engagement rings were not the end-product of a system based on African forced labor for the profit of bloody diamond lords. As a result, Tiffany upped its supervision of the mines in places such as Botswana, Namibia or Russia, all of which provide its stones.

In the world of socially and politically-active corporations, conscientious consumers have a significant say in the values that companies choose to follow

---

[59] "What Is Tiffany Doing About The Problem Of Conflict Diamonds?" Tiffany, accessed January 3rd 2019, https://www.tiffany.com/faq/a-tiffany-diamond-faq/what-is-tiffany-doing-about-the-problem-of-conflict-diamond/.

– even if the guiding reason of the latter is driving sales upwards. Consumers have the chance to use the self-interested behavior of corporations, profit-seeking ventures, to their own goals, just like the Founding Fathers of the United States decided to deal with interest groups by pitting them against one another – a process in which free speech was paramount. The global diamond industry has, traditionally, been one in which transparency was not valued. Gold and diamonds have been fought over by kings and emperors for millennia, but nowadays progressive consumers want not just the end-product, but the guarantee that their money did not go toward unsavory sources – and their wishes go a long way.

After the openness initiative from the part of the corporation, Tiffany's customers now know the entire route of the diamonds they buy, from the African mines to the Belgian sorters and then to the polishing and cutting factories in Vietnam or Mauritius, before finally arriving in the store. By asserting control over its supply chain, Tiffany, a New York-based company, is also imposing new regulation on producers from Africa and Asia in a way that governments – for all their power – could not do. The self-interested company which would obviously earn more by hiding the source of its cheaper diamonds is taking a responsible stance, driving business away from warlords and empowering legitimate enterprises based on regulation, all because its consumers are willing to pay more in order to make the world a better place.

13. Nike, Colin Kaepernick and the right to protest

The autumn of 2018 started off with a commercial campaign unlike any other, one which intended to sell shoes and sneakers but which nevertheless rocked the political environment of the flagship of modern liberal democracy, the United States of America. The campaign was initiated by the multinational corporation and one of the best-known brands in footwear, Nike, and it featured former N.F.L. star Colin Kaepernick.

While a sportsman appearing in a Nike commercial was nothing new, the campaign in question was different, as ever since 2016 Kaepernick was the face of an extremely visible movement that protested police brutality against African-Americans. The former quarterback, who used to kneel while the United States anthem was being played before every game as a sign of protest, was left without a contract with any team within the N.F.L. Simply put, no team would hire him. As such, he signed a multiyear deal with Nike. Kaepernick's face soon appeared on an ad with the message "Believe in something. Even if it means sacrificing everything."[60] The political message sent by Nike simply by the act of hiring Kaepernick alone was doubled by a clear commitment to his previous protest. Nike was against police brutality.

The backlash was immediate. Social media and political talk shows were awash with commentaries regarding the ad. People identifying with the right of the political spectrum in the U.S. vowed to boycott Nike. Some even posted videos and images of themselves burning their Nike apparel and using the tag "#JustBurnIt," mocking Nike's well-known line "Just Do It."[61]

Before signing with Kaepernick, however, Nike also secured another deal – with the National Football League. In this way, the company secured deals with 32 teams to provide them with uniforms for their games, with the logo branded on every one. The company was playing a political game and it was doing it marvelously.

Media-wise, Nike's Kaepernick campaign was a hit. While many contested it, similar or perhaps greater numbers came in full support of the move. While some burned their shoes, others rushed to buy even more Nike apparel.[62] President Trump, who had previously criticized the protest of Kaepernick and others for being disrespectful to the flag and to the American troops, also responded to Nike's commercial, saying it sends "a terrible message." On the other hand, Trump also recognized that "this is what this country is all about, that you have certain freedoms to do things that other people think you shouldn't do."[63] Nike was enjoying its American freedoms, according to Trump.

In this way, the president, who styled himself a defender of free speech, along with other conservatives that typically oppose political correctness, equated the right to free speech of Colin Kaepernick to that of Nike, a corporation now endowed with artificial personhood. Looked at in another way, Nike – through its money – was making Kaepernick's speech possible, and in doing so it was

[60] Kevin Draper and Ken Belson, "Colin Kaepernick, Face of N.F.L. Protests, Is Face of New Nike Campaign," *The New York Times*, September 3rd, 2018, https://www.nytimes.com/2018/09/03/sports/kaepernick-nike.html.

[61] Marina Nazario and Dylan Roach, "Nike's incredible road to becoming the world's dominant sneaker retailer," *Business Insider*, October 4th, 2015, https://www.businessinsider.com.au/nike-history-timeline-2015-10.

[62] Ed Mazza, "Haters mocked for wrecking their stuff to protest Kaepernick deal," *Huffington Post*, September 9th, 2018, https://www.huffpost.com/entry/nike-colin-kaepernick-protest_n_5.

[63] Julia Horowitz, "Trump: Nike's Clin Kaepernick campaign sends 'terrible message'," *CNN*, September 4th, 2018, https://money.cnn.com/2018/09/04/news/companies/trump-nike-kaepernick/index.html.

taking a political stance of its own, not unlike how individual donors make the political speech of candidates possible through contributions.

In *The Atlantic*, Hunt begins by noting that "it's significant that an institution as powerful as Nike has thrown its weight behind Kaepernick and his crusade against racial injustice."[64] What is essentially the marketing move of a profit-seeking company is now easily confounded with the political statement of a quasi-sentient artificial being which, due to its financial power and market notoriety, can throw its weight behind a certain camp within a political debate. Whether or not Nike's apparent support of Kaepernick will be beneficial to his initial cause, that of protesting police brutality against African-Americans, it cannot be denied that the campaign initiated by the footwear company is keeping the issue alive and ensures that the debate continues.

Nike is only one of the large multinationals that decided to tackle racial injustice – at least for marketing purposes. Thirty years ago, however, the same company was accused of subjecting its workers in Indonesia to inhuman and often dangerous working conditions. Back then, Nike only gave in after unions such as the Worker Rights Consortium appeared in its factories.[65] Nike came to the negotiations table and in 2001, the sports apparel brand finally embraced that a corporation of its size had to act with social responsibility. For Hunt, supporting Kaepernick is for Nike "simply good business," with even the negative reactions stirring more interest for the brand itself. However, such pointed criticism from Hunt and other commentators of the new politically-mindful corporations centers around the act of taking a stance, while missing the shift in the political and economic framework that is taking place due to it. Even if it is only for mere financial gains and increased sales, companies are nevertheless stepping into what was, traditionally, the place of the "political animal," the "natural" person, men and women. Nike now has identifiably liberal stances, even if just for appealing to the more liberally-minded consumers out there. In itself, that is an entirely new development.

Other voices criticized the practice of connecting a product to a certain value. Trevor Noah, host of the late-night *Daily Show*, essentially a politically-charged comedy show, argued that "people shouldn't put their alignment behind brands. Buy the shoe because you like the shoe, not because it represents my political beliefs, because I don't know if it completely does. Nike might do

---

[64] Joshua Hunt, "Colin Kaepernick, Nike, and the myth of good and bad companies," *The Atlantic*, September 5th, 2018, https://www.theatlantic.com/business/archive/2018/09/nike-kaepernick/569371/.

[65] Tim Conor, "Time to scale up cooperation? Trade associations, NGOs, and the International Anti-Sweatshop Movement," *Development in Practice* 14, 1/2, (February 2004): pp. 61-70 doi:10.1080/0961452032000170631.

things you don't like."[66] His assessment is perfectly reasonable – but the same could be said about any representative, any politician running for office. If the market is wide and populated enough for consumers to afford to avoid a brand, irrespective of its size, *why wouldn't consumers align financially to the brand that represents their moral values?* In the end, the same result is achieved – one's ideas, values and stances on different issues are represented. Moreover, the cost incurred by consumers for aligning their daily shopping with their beliefs is low or zero, considering the interchangeability of products and the fierce competition in the developed world, Nike may not act on abortion in the same liberal fashion as it has against racial injustice, but neither would a Democratic governor or candidate necessarily hold a coherently liberal stance over every issue.

Noah says that "we will go crazy with people tracking down the political ideology of every single item they buy," but consumers and voters, being the same, already do that – or try to do it – with their elected representatives, even those they did not vote for themselves. Noah's argument against corporate involvement in politics could therefore easily be interpreted as an argument against democratic participation, such as "issues are too complex for most people to be able to follow." Realistically, one cannot keep track of the values of every company behind every product in a supermarket, just like a voter cannot be expected to know the opinions on everything of each candidate in an election. Just like in politics, a tag, working as a shortcut, will do the job. A politically-minded consumer would, therefore, only need to know that Nike is liberal. Its competitors may want, just like a party, to fill the value-void by moving to a more conservative side of the spectrum.

Nike's Kaepernick campaign received criticism and applause, both amounting to free-of-charge publicity and exposure worth 43 million dollars, according to an Apex Media Group analysis cited by *The Hill*.[67] In an analysis that took into account only online sales – which have seen a rise on their own, independent of any other factor – it was shown that following the Kaepernick campaign, Nike's revenues were higher than a year before. After an initial drop,

[66] The Daily Show with Trevor Noah, "Nike's Kaepernick Ad – Between the Scenes," YouTube video, 2:05, September 5th 2018, https://www.youtube.com/watch?v=nma4GJ2rfwU&ab_channel=TheDailyShowwithTrevorNoah.
[67] Aris Folley, "Nike's online sales surge after Kaepernick ads revealed," *The Hill*, September 7th, 2018, https://thehill.com/blogs/blog-briefing-room/news/405633-nikes-online-sales-surge-after-kaepernick-ads-revealed-report.

Nike's online sales rebounded to much higher levels, growing 31% - compared to 17% in the same period of 2017.[68] The gamble was paying off.

As more time passed and the number of ads featuring former NFL player Colin Kaepernick kept increasing, Nike's overall sales also went up. Since its first Kaepernick ad, the corporation racked up sales of 61% more items of clothing being sold out, and with its stock – after an initial drop – reaching new highs.[69] By September of 2018, Nike's shares had gone up to $85.67, amounting to a 36% rise, making it the top performer in Dow's index of 30 blue-chip stocks.[70] Nike's campaign shows that for a profit-seeking corporation, adopting a politically-charged, divisive stance can be profitable.

In a style reminiscent of Georgia's Lieutenant governor, Casey Cagle, and his threat made against airliner Delta, the mayor of Kenner, a town in New Orleans, also decided to boycott Nike, banning the company's products from being purchased by the local booster clubs. Almost a week later, however, the same mayor, facing protests and rallies led by NFL players from the New Orleans Saints, decided to go back on his decision. In his words, the entire affair had "placed Kenner in a false and unflattering light."[71] The mayor ended with a vow to always safeguard his patriotism but to move on to other projects. The voice of the corporation – and its consumer allies – proved dominant once again.

14. Corporations and abortion

Corporations that have taken the initiative with regard to social issues that affect women offer the counter example. An example is Gucci, which chose to take a stance on abortion. In its new Cruise 2020 collection, Gucci featured feminist slogans and imagery on its clothes, such as the phrase "My Body My Choice."[72] The same collection features a grown with an embroidered uterus added on the front. This is nothing new for Gucci, as back in 2013 the brand

---

[68] "Nike Sales Grew 31% During Labor Day Weekend and Kaepernick Ad Campaign," *Edison Trends*, September 7th, 2018, https://trends.edison.tech/research/nike-labor-day-2018.html.

[69] Jharonne Martis, "Nike ad spurs 61% rise in sold out items," *Refinitiv*, September 19th, 2018, https://lipperalpha.refinitiv.com/2018/09/nike-ad-spurs-61-rise-in-sold-out-items/.

[70] Kate Gibson, "Colin Kaepernick is Nike's $6 billion man," CBS News, September 21th, 2018, https://www.cbsnews.com/news/colin-kaepernick-nike-6-billion-man/.

[71] Josh Hafner, "Louisiana mayor rescinds Nike ban after blowback from community and advice from attorney," *USA Today*, September 14th, 2018, https://eu.usatoday.com/story/money/nation-now/2018/09/13/nike-ban-mayor-dropped-louisiana-advice-city-attorney/1292137002/.

[72] Aris Folley, "Gucci advocates for women's rights to abortion on the runway," *The Hill*, May 29th, 2019, https://thehill.com/blogs/in-the-know/in-the-know/446067-gucci-advocates-for-womens-rights-to-abortion-on-the-runway.

founded the "Chime for Change" nonprofit campaign meant to advocate for gender equality and reproductive rights on a global scale. Other issues that Gucci plans to tackle are maternal health, individual choice, helping underprivileged communities and women activists in the Middle East.

Why would Gucci take up women's issues? Because the vast majority of its consumer base is made out of women, and its brand is built on women's clothing. By connecting its name to social and even political campaigns meant to aid women, Gucci can obtain an advantage against *silent* competitors such as Dolce & Gabbana, Armani, Louis Vuitton, Prada, Yves Saint Lauren and others. Those consumers who are actively aware of such issues will reward Gucci with their purchases, while no opposing group exists.

Gucci was not the only corporation that chose to speak about abortion. In the fall of 2019, Georgia's Republican governor, Brian Kemp, signed a bill that banned abortion if the heartbeat of the fetus could be detected. As that usually happens around the sixth week of pregnancy, the bill was viewed by women's rights groups as a grossly unjust and restrictive. A year earlier, Kemp had defeated the Democratic hopeful, Stacy Abrams, by a very small margin, gathering 50.2% of the votes to Stacy's 48.8%. Not unlike many elected representatives before him, Kemp could hardly claim to have the people of Georgia behind him as he signed controversial measures into law – this time, the "heartbeat" bill.

The response did not linger. Activists challenged the bill and protested, but corporations took a stand as well. Netflix, Disney, NBCUniversal and WarnerMedia, giants of the entertainment industry who preferred Georgia due to the tax breaks it offered to filmmakers, threatened to stop producing movies and shows in Georgia if the bill became law.[73] Foregoing present tax incentives, the corporations were looking on the long-term, judging the costs of associating their names with the restrictive abortion law. Employing liberal stars and catering to a young, movie-going audience or depending on monthly subscriptions, like Netflix, these corporations could not afford to be deaf to the protests of their patrons and employees. Kemp, on the other hand, safely did so, protected by the two-year governor mandate and the proven short-term memory of the electorate.

In a statement for the press, Netflix said that "we have many women working on productions in Georgia, whose rights, along with millions of others, will be severely restricted by this law [...]should it ever come into effect, *we*'d rethink

---

[73] Brian Stelter and Shannon Liao, "Disney, Netflix and WarnerMedia say new abortion law may push their movies out of Georgia," *CNN Business*, May 30th, 2019, https://edition.cnn.com/2019/05/30/business/disney-bob-iger-abortion-georgia/index.html.

our entire investment in Georgia."[74] A similar message came from NBCUniversal and AT&T's WarnerMedia, which employs thousands in Georgia and its CNN headquarters in Atlanta. Speaking for Disney, its CEO noted that if the "heartbeat bill" becomes law, "many people who work for us will not want to work there [...] We will have to heed their wishes."[75] Employing thousands and bringing billions into Georgia, the corporations spoke with a booming voice, whereas ACLU and other women's rights groups could only exert a limited pressure on the Republican governor. In October 2019, however, a federal judge temporarily blocked the bill,[76] which was supposed to take effect at the start of 2020, allowing the two camps to continue confronting and threatening each other.

15. Danone and Social Responsibility

Some corporations have taken the idea of a socially responsible and responsive business further than most. Danone, the well-known French company that commercializes dairy products in 120 markets and which racked up sales worth €24.7 billion in 2017,[77] is especially aware of the trends among new consumers – the millennials, most of all. In response to politically-motivated brand boycotts and a clear turn toward organic and locally-produced goods, Danone, through the voice of its current CEO, Emmanuel Faber, has explicitly moved its aim away from creating shareholder value and towards creating a greater benefit for consumers. In a way, this is a continuation of Danone's history – in 1972, just four years after the 1968 student protests in France and Germany, which spread left-leaning ideas of solidarity through the European and North-American society, the same company was proclaiming to pursue both economic and social goals.[78] "Corporate responsibility does not end at the factory gate or the office door," said Danone CEO Antoine Riboud in a speech given in front of 2000 executives gathered in Marseille.[79] The company became

---

[74] "Netflix will 'rethink' Georgia shoots if abortion law holds," *AP News*, May 28th, 2019, https://apnews.com/82bc083f3131474b9643ac870b30010b.

[75] "Georgia abortion: WarnerMedia joins Disney and Netflix in considering options," *BBC News*, May 30th, 2019, https://www.bbc.com/news/entertainment-arts-48457401/.

[76] Alexandra Desanctis, "Judge Blocks Georgia's Pro-Life Heartbeat Bill," *National Review*, October 1st, 2019, https://www.nationalreview.com/corner/judge-blocks-georgia-heartbeat-bill/.

[77] "Danone – One Planet, One Hope," Danone, accessed March 17th 2019, https://www.danone.com/integrated-annual-report-2019.html.

[78] "A walk through Danone's history," *Medium*, November 21st, 2016, https://medium.com/@Danone/a-walk-through-the-danones-history-a031acdb7335.

[79] "Danone's dual commitment to business success and social progress," Danone Communities, accessed December 5th 2019, http://prod.danone.emakina.nbs-test.com/.

committed to environmental protection, better health through food and sustainability.

In line with the desires of its target consumers, Danone has been opening smaller subsidiaries which produce biscuits and chocolate all over Europe, all in an effort to be local in relation to every market. At the same time, the company is striving to become greener, opting for recycled plastic bottles for its Evian water. In Bangladesh, Danone provides high-quality, cheap yoghurt to children.

All of Danone's strides went toward obtaining a certification as an ethical, socially-responsible and environmentally-friendly company, a "B Corporation," a label created by an independent movement called B Lab. Like many other organizations which monitor corporations and their practices – Sleeping Giants is another example, in a different field of activity – B Lab seeks to steer corporations away from merely obtaining profits and toward serving society in ethical ways. By 2030, Danone seeks to obtain the certification for all its subsidiaries, prompting millennials in America – the American supermarket chain Wal-Mart being Danone's biggest single customer – and Europe to buy more Danone products.[80] In effect, Danone is trying to convince its potential customers to buy its products not because they are much cheaper or healthier than those of competitors – but because of who Danone is and what it stands for.

But Danone's ethical approach also had an economic background. By 2017, not unlike Gillette before its progressive turn, the company was in economic trouble – with a low 8% return on its capital investments – and was thus forced to radically change tactics. One year later, 12 financial backers had signed a deal with Danone, giving the company a credit of €2bn tied to its certification as a "B Corporation."[81]

Danone's story is telling for a new trend made obvious by the several stories presented in this chapter – corporations are transforming, but they are doing so in order to protect their original goal, namely that of registering profits. In a global market suffocated by large-scale competitors offering interchangeable products, the only way in which a brand can differentiate itself from its competitors is through means that are social, environmental and even political in nature.

---

[80] "Danone rethinks the idea of the firm," *The Economist*, August 9th, 2018, https://www.economist.com/business/2018/08/09/danone-rethinks-the-idea-of-the-firm.

[81] "Danone rethinks the idea of the firm," https://www.economist.com/business/2018/08/09/danone-rethinks-the-idea-of-the-firm.

16. Peloton and Sexism

When they release an ad, corporations may not be able to tell how consumers will interpret it. When fitness equipment maker Peloton released its new Christmas commercial, "the gift that gives," in early December, it was certainly unable to foresee the storm that it would cause. The TV spot featured a woman who, upon receiving a Peloton stationary bike from her husband, decides to keep a video diary dedicated to him showing her efforts and progress. Enraged critics sprang up and argued that the story made it seem that the woman was being pressured to keep her weight under control and that she was obediently doing so for her husband, who had no issue skipping any exercise.[82] To them, the ad depicted a sexist and classist story of oppression and diverging fitness standards for men and women.

The comments section of social media platforms may not seem essential to business, but it is no doubt the public square in which concerns are voiced and where social debates are held. The reality of this hit Peloton when the value of its shares fell by more than 9% in a single day, representing $942 million in market value.[83]

Not long ago Peloton had been a promising startup that spelled healthy living as a business model, but now the company was being associated with sexism and described as "the fancy indoor-cycling company for the one percent."[84] This prompted the downward trend of Peloton to continue, causing its losses to go up to $1.5 billion in market value just a few days later. Asked by the media, market analysts shrugged in surprise and said that the continued drop, unexpected for a company that had gone public recently and had previously seen a sustained growth, could only be due to the ad.[85] The brand itself had become toxic, synonymous to patriarchy, and the actors appearing in its ad – the "Peloton Husband" in particular – tried to distance themselves from it as

---

[82] Joshua Fineman, "Peloton stock is pummeled on backlash from 'gift that gives' ad," *Fortune*, December 4th, 2019, https://fortune.com/2019/12/04/peloton-stock-falls-after-backlash-gift-that-gives-ad/.

[83] Carmen Reinicke, "Peloton saw $942 million in market value wiped out in a single day amid backlash to its controversial holiday ad," *Business Insider*, December 4th, 2019, https://markets.businessinsider.com/news/stocks/pelotons-stock-price-plummet-wiped-942-million-market-value-holiday-ad-2019-12-1028737428.

[84] Devon Ivie, "The Peloton Husband Is Worried That His Acting Career Is Dead," *Vulture*, December 8th, 2019, https://www.vulture.com/2019/12/peloton-ad-husband-is-worried-that-his-acting-career-is-dead.html.

[85] Megan Cerullo, "Peloton ad costs the company and shareholders $1.6 billion," *CBS News*, December 4th, 2019, https://www.cbsnews.com/news/peloton-bike-ad-even-wall-street-hates-the-controversial-peloton-bike-ad-today-2019-12-05/.

well.[86] They had been the face of Peloton, *its speech*, and were naturally associated with the message.

Finally, representatives of the Peloton stated that it is monitoring the market backlash and that it is considering pulling the ad altogether. The Peloton episode shows that corporations can no longer afford to ignore their own voice and conduct business as usual. Their image and products do not exist in a void, but in a politicized market that is foretelling of the future corporate democratic system. Until then, however, Peloton *spoke* – even unwittingly – and the consumers did not like what they heard.

But the story does not stop there. Actor Ryan Reynolds took to the stage, employing the "Peloton Wife" actress to make a video depicting her toasting to "new beginnings" together with friends.[87] Reynolds' video, however, was not made purely for fun – it was made to promote his own brand of drinks, Aviation Gin.

What was really happening? A company was climbing on top of another's failure in order to promote itself, carefully inserting its own products – gin – into the unfolding story surrounding Peloton's mistake. No critic stepped up to argue that Aviation Gin was trying to extract commercial success for itself out of the anti-sexist rage against the fitness equipment maker's ad, even though that is exactly what it was doing. Instead, the ad for Aviation Gin received praise for being creative and well-timed. In the new market, being rewarded for a "creative and well-timed" ad – corporate speech – that strikes all the right cords in terms of moral and social values is to be considered absolutely legitimate.

The carrot and the stick are therefore both in place when it comes to the relation between consumers and corporations. The former is showcased by Aviation Gin's experience, which profited in terms of reputation and sales, while the latter describes the dangerous market waters in which Peloton found itself.

Outcomes

What were the results of the socio-political ventures of the progressive corporations? One possible indicator would be stock market value, as it factors in a multitude of variables such as present and projected sales, growth potential, assets and a general impression regarding the company's future.

---

[86] Cerullo, "Peloton ad."

[87] Owen Daughtery, "Ryan Reynolds recruits actress from Peloton ad to troll fitness company's controversial commercial," *The Hill*, December 7th, 2019, https://thehill.com/blogs/in-the-know/in-the-know/473510-ryan-reynolds-recruits-actress-from-peloton-ad-to-troll-fitness.

1. Gillette's toxic masculinity ad began running on the 14th of January 2019. Almost one year later, the common stock value of its parent company, Procter & Gamble, went from $91.15 per share at last call to $124.51,[88] a 33% increase in value. Unilever, the parent company of The Dollar Shave Club since 2016, which refrained from producing divisive, politically-charged ads, saw its monthly stock value go from $52 to $60 in the same time period, a 15% increase – not to mention that around 15-20 million Unilever shares are usually traded on the New York Stock Exchange every month, with a 76-million high point in September 2019, while P&G shares are traded in monthly volumes of 150 million, with a high point of 785 million in September 2019.

2. After its commitment to rid its shelves of "blood diamonds," Tiffany's stock market value went from $79.35 per share in January 2019 to $123.90 in October of 2019,[89] a 56% increase in value.

3. From September 2018, when the Kaepernick ad started running, until October 2019, Nike's stock market value per share went from $79.39 at last call to $90,[90] representing a 13% increase. Adidas, an important albeit smaller competitor to Nike, the undisputed market leader in global sports footwear, starts at $124 in the same period and sees an almost constant increase to $156 in October 2019, a 25.8% total increase.[91] One must keep in mind, however, that Nike shares, like those of P&G, are traded in huge volumes, around 150 million each month, while Adidas has only about a million or so shares change hands every month. The only major hiccup for Adidas came in January 2019, when its stocks hit a low point of $105. Importantly, in the same month Adidas was forced

---

[88] "Procter and Gamble (PG) NYSE historical data," Nasdaq, accessed November 20th 2019, https://www.nasdaq.com/market-activity/stocks/pg/historical.

[89] "Tiffany and Co. (TIF) NYSE," Nasdaq, accessed November 2nd 2019, https://www.nasdaq.com/market-activity/stocks/tif.

[90] "Nike Inc. (NKE) NYSE," Nasdaq, accessed November 1st 2019, https://www.nasdaq.com/market-activity/stocks/nke/historical.

[91] "Adidas (ADDYY) NYSE," Nasdaq, accessed November 1st 2019, https://www.nasdaq.com/market-activity/stocks/addyy/historical.

to remove a pair of all-white shoes that were intended to honor Black History Month[92] following public complaints.

4. On May 16th 2020, as summer was kicking off, Nike's market share price reached a low point of $67.45. In the grip of a pandemic and forced indoors, Americans stopped buying sports apparel. On May 29th, the company launched its "For Once, Don't Do It" ad condemning police violence. Simple words on a black background, the ad said "For once, don't do it. Don't pretend there's not a problem in America. Don't turn your back on racism. Don't accept innocent lives being taken from us. Don't make any more excuses. Don't think this doesn't affect you. Don't sit back and be silent. Don't think you can't be part of the change. Let's all be part of the change," followed by the Nike logo, eerily similar to the "I approve this message"-type ads that political candidates put out in every election. The ad did not feature a single Nike product. In June 2020, Nike pledged $40 million to black community organizations.[93] On July 30th, Nike also put out another ad featuring black, disabled, LGBT, women and Muslim sportspeople.[94] On September 7th, Nike's market share price was $118, a 75% increase from May.

Of course, such measurements and comparisons must be treated extensively in following studies with proper indicators such as stock market volatility, volumes traded, net income, total value and general market conditions taken into account. Overall sector conditions and outlook weigh much heavier in this respect. Still, it is not far-fetched to state that it is economically profitable for corporations to act as political agents, to tie their brand to a side of the political spectrum, the progressive side.

---

[92] Samantha McDonald, "Adidas pulls 'black history month' sneakers amid 'all-white' color criticism," *FootWearNews*, February 1st, 2019, https://footwearnews.com/2019/focus/athletic-outdoor/adidas-back-history-month-sneakers-cbc-pulled-1202737846/.
[93] Alexandra Kelley, "Nike Inc. announces $40 million donation to black community organizations," *The Hill*, June 5th, 2020, https://thehill.com/changing-america/respect/equality/501369-nike-inc-announces-40-million-donation-to-black-community?fbclid=IwAR27LrLkX0HoXwAtPXTR16xQUhTVM5qwD0NcQxFnDKm5gKu3K2hfCFieYLo.
[94] Nike, "You Can't Stop Us," YouTube video, 1:30, July 30th 2020, https://www.youtube.com/watch?v=WA4dDs0T7sMandab_channel=Nike.

Chapter X

Free Speech and Corporations

If the previous chapter dealt with individual cases of corporations engaging in societal debates and taking sides on divisive issues, the present one deals with a grander topic that concerns the power of corporations in particular – free speech. One can safely say that the 2016 presidential elections in the United States have polarized the American public to a larger degree than similar electoral competitions in the past few decades. However, it is also true that social media, bringing people in front of each other constantly, has also enabled debates and differences of opinion to become more visible. Liberals and conservatives might have had debates of the same intensity in the 1910s as well, but it is only now that they can condemn each other directly, encouraged by a feud-thirsty virtual audience, while at the same time enjoying the cover of anonymity.

In the higher spheres of politics, however, the recognition of the impact of social media on elections particularly and on the political domain generally has already passed into common knowledge. Making extensive use of social media turned Barack Obama's 2008 campaign manager into a superstar of the field. Now, it is the political coloring and leanings of these corporate-facilitated platforms – Facebook and Twitter primarily – that has become the subject of political and scholarly and public attention. In August of 2018, Donald Trump Jr., son of Republican president Donald J. Trump, argued that conservatives should have their own Facebook-like platform.[1] His comments came in the wake of a declaration of some 100 Facebook employees, joined in a group called "FB'ers for Political Diversity," that deplored the "political monoculture" at the tech giant and argued for ideological diversity in an environment that was dense with liberal values. Not long after, the 45th president of the United States himself became involved with the subject, arguing – not without irony - in an August 18th tweet that "social media is totally discriminating against

---

[1] Megan Keller, "Trump Jr. says he'd back a new conservative version of Facebook," *The Hill*, May 30th, 2018, https://thehill.com/policy/technology/404326-trump-jr-says-hed-back-a-new-conservative-version-of-facebook.

Republican/Conservative voices."[2] It was no longer about how politicians and candidates could reach voters – it was about how the social media platforms had turned into radically empowered and politically-inclined actors.

Aside from their active role in the debates, social media platforms are also the preferred agora in which political discourse takes place. Modern mass democracy turned to representatives because it was physically impossible for all citizens to be present in a "town square." However, platforms such as Facebook and Twitter come to partially solve that problem – a Democrat in Michigan can pick a fight with a Republican in Texas at any point in time, all due to the wondrous comments section.

Scandals can spark out at any point and live out their minutes of fame entirely on social media; some of them can even involve corporations, even when governmental policies or legislative acts are not part of the concern. After posting a number of racist tweets resulting in the cancellation of her eponymous show, Roseanne Barr blamed the sleep aid Ambien, saying that she was "Ambien tweeting."[3] In response, the maker of Ambien, the pharmaceutical company Sanofi, issued a statement saying that "while all pharmaceutical treatments have side effects, racism is not a known side effect of any Sanofi medication" and that "people of all races, religions and nationalities work at Sanofi every day to improve the lives of people around the world."[4] Sanofi was quick to denounce any connection between itself and its products and racism for the same reason that the airline companies distanced themselves from the policy of separating migrant families – the consumer market would have punished them. Large corporations that touch the lives of millions of people every day can no longer afford to be politically neutral – on certain issues or even in general.

When they are not taking part in the debates or ensuring a platform for them, social media companies take on the mantle of regulators of speech. In September of 2018, after a week-long "time out," Twitter permanently banned conspiracy theory-peddler Alex Jones due to his violating of website policies. Following the ban, Jones' own website saw a massive decrease in traffic, signaling the importance of social media visibility even for a name that was

---

[2] Kate Conger and Sheera Frenkel, "Dozens at Facebook unite to challenge its 'intolerant' liberal culture," *The New York Times*, August 28th, 2018, https://www.nytimes.com/2018/08/28/technology/inside-facebook-employees-political-bias.html.

[3] Michael Nedelmann, "Ambien maker Sanofi: 'Racism is not a known side effect," *CNN*, May 30th, 2018, https://edition.cnn.com/2018/05/30/health/ambien-roseanne-barr-racist-tweets-bn/index.html.

[4] Nedelmann, "Ambien maker Sanofi."

well-established in its niche market of viewers. Kicked out of the digital agora, Jones' speech was practically curtailed to a large extent.

Jones was not the first conservative to be banned by tech giants from their social media platforms. In 2016, then-editor for Breitbart News, itself an outlet blamed for spreading fake news, Milo Yiannopoulos was also banned. Tim Gionet, another far-right voice, formerly working for BuzzFeed, was also banned. "De-platforming," as it has been called, can thus be seen as extremely effective in reducing the voice of a public personality, especially since, like in Jones' case, Twitter served as the link between his off-putting tweets and the national news outlets and political talk shows. Discussing his latest conspiracy theory on national news meant his channel received waves of attention which, in turn, brought the conservative talk show host revenue.[5]

On Fox News, the conservative-leaning television station, titles such as "Tech Tyranny," written in blood-red, throne behind talk-show hosts. People like Tucker Carlson often state that tech companies stifle the speech of conservatives and decry the state of modern democracy, where corporations get to regulate speech, trampling on traditional values.[6]

While liberals pressured Facebook and Twitter to curtail hate speech and fake news outlets, the same social media platforms quickly incurred the wrath of an unexpected segment of the population – elected officials and representatives of the government. After permanently banning conservative talk show host Alex Jones, a move which received cheers from liberals, tech giants and multinational corporations Facebook and Twitter received a two-line warning from the Justice Department, which said that the ban, along with other acts, may be "intentionally stifling free exchange of ideas,"[7] particularly conservative ones.

Without specifying whether or not it was pursuing legal action, the Justice Department followed a line set by President Donald Trump and his allies, all of whom readily took up the claim that tech giants were biased against the right of the political spectrum. Caught between criticisms of its inaction regarding

---

[5] Taylor Lorenz, "The End Finally Comes for Alex Jones," *The Atlantic,* September 7th, 2018, https://www.theatlantic.com/technology/archive/2018/09/the-end-finally-comes-for-alex-jones/569578/.
[6] Tucker Carlson, "Tucker Carlson: Big Business Hates Your Family - National Conservatism Conference," YouTube video, 53:37 minutes, July 18th 2019, https://www.youtube.com/watch?v=AXGoWtK1NnY&ab_channel=NationalConservatism.
[7] Craig Timberg, Tony Romm, Devlin Barrett and Brian Fung, "Justice Department warns tech companies as Facebook and Twitter defend themselves in Congress," *The Washington Post,* September 6th, 2018, https://www.washingtonpost.com/technology/2018/09/05/justice-department-consider-allegations-censorship-facebook-twitter/.

fake news – inaction which was taken by liberals to mean an endorsement – and the revenge of a conservative government, Facebook, Twitter, Google and other large tech companies are put in an awkward position of facilitating communication – and thus, democratic deliberation – while attempting to remain politically neutral.

The threat of politically-involved corporations has had spectacular ideological effects on both the left and the right. Liberals, historically weary of big business and their vast financial resources and private interests, have been cheering progressive advents of corporate giants in numerous industries. On the other side, conservatives, historically champions of the free market and of the minimal state, have been increasingly supportive of regulating multinationals. Each side, however, has its own "good corporations" and "bad corporations" – for the conservatives, the gun-manufacturers and energy industry were good; for the liberals, the technology industry and the entertainment industry fulfilled the same role.

The ubiquitous nature of social media also means that corporations, like politicians, are permanently under the public eye. One act of the corporation can be made public and magnified, put on the screens of hundreds of millions in a single day. In 2017, right-wing activists, including white supremacists, marched in Charlottesville in the *Unite the Right* rally. Hundreds of people showed up and clashes between them and the police or counter-protesters ensued. In 2018, only 20 to 30 people attended the same rally. Part of the reason is that immediately after the Charlottesville rally, the described "Nazis" that marched with torches in 2017 were being identified through social media and pressure was exerted upon their employers in order to fire them. Smaller brands were again at the forefront – Mojo Burrito, a restaurant in Tennessee, fired Terrance Hightower, citing that it "does not condone harassment, racism or discrimination of any kind;"[8] Uno Pizzeria in Vermont fired Ryan Roy for the same reason, saying the company is "committed to the fair treatment of all people;"[9] Nigel Krofta was fired by South Carolina's Limehouse & Sons after he appeared in pictures at the rally, the firm saying that it "does not condone the actions of the people involved in this horrific display."[10]

The micro-blogging platform Twitter, the preferred method of communication by U.S. president Donald Trump, is also a corporation – a Silicon Valley firm that caters to younger generations and which is staffed by

---

[8] Naomi LaChance, "More Nazis are Getting Identified and Fired after Charlottesville," *Huffington Post,* August 16th, 2017, https://www.huffpost.com/entry/more-nazis-are-getting-identified-and-fired-after-charlottesville_b_599477dbe4b0eef7ad2c0318.

[9] LaChance, "More Nazis are Getting Identified."

[10] LaChance, "More Nazis are Getting Identified."

them. In August of 2018, in the aftermath of the week-long "pause" given to far-right radio host Alex Jones by Apple, YouTube, Facebook and Spotify for hate speech, Twitter CEO Jack Dorsey admitted that the employees of Twitter "share a largely left-leaning bias"[11] but that the company itself operates without bias, judging behavior and not content. Nevertheless, Dorsey's confession sparked the outrage of conservatives all over the United States, which claimed – not without merit – that they had been right about the fact that the new regulators of speech were biased themselves.

Ideological bias within corporations that oversee social media platforms, the modern-day political equivalents of the Greek agoras, has been widely discussed and even accepted. Dorsey admitted that the "conservative-leaning folks" working at Twitter may have felt "silenced by [...] what they perceive to be the broader percentage of leanings within the company."[12] At the same time, he argued that Twitter should be as inclusive as possible to employees with different political opinions.

While impacting politics through campaign contributions and even drafting of laws, corporations are also witnessing a process of *bottom-up politicization* and *top-down reaction*. The new development is that employees, just as consumers, want their employer to behave and agree with their own ideological worldview and values, and not just provide a stable workplace and a monthly check. This inward-originating pressure couples with the external influence of consumers rewarding or punishing corporations through their purchases, depending on their own ideological standing and the one assumed by the corporate person. Beyond that, corporations pushing an employee and consumer-demanded political agenda – as in the case of silencing a right-wing conspiracy theorist – might, in turn, incur the outrage of politicians and elected representatives within the same side, or the opposing one, of the political spectrum. This is the new reality of the market – not only an economic one, but also an entrenched political dimension to the act of producing, commercializing and purchasing. When the product in discussion is an online social space where speech is produced and circulated, the issue only becomes graver.

---

[11] John Bowden, "Twitter CEO Jack Dorsey: I 'fully admit' our bias is 'more left-leaning'," *The Hill*, August 18th, 2018, https://thehill.com/policy/technology/402495-twitter-ceo-jack-dorsey-i-fully-admit-our-bias-is-more-left-leaning.

[12] Megan Keller, "Twitter CEO Jack Dorsey: Conservative employees don't feel safe to express their opinions," *The Hill*, September 16th, 2018, https://thehill.com/policy/technology/406927-twitter-ceo-jack-dorsey-conservative-employees-dont-feel-safe-to-express.

This chapter has argued that with social media giants such as Twitter and Facebook, political speech is a given. When Twitter allows fringe, right-wing propaganda, it takes a certain side – but also when it bans it, enraging and satisfying swaths of users (consumers) with every decision. Social media companies not only speak, but control speech as well. The next chapter deals with a wiz of social media, an elected representative criticized for creating and spreading more fake news than perhaps any major political figure in recent democratic history, namely Donald Trump.

Chapter XI

Trump vs. Corporations

Twitter's employees may have a left-leaning bias, but the social media platform also served as an effective megaphone for Donald Trump's conservative messaging. Trump's relationship with corporations is similar to the Manichean approach which dominates much of his thinking – he likes the "good ones," which create jobs in the U.S. and steer clear from politics, and disdains the "bad ones," which are ran by people he dislikes or which have acted against him in some way. The same 45th president of the United States has never backed away from directly criticizing corporations even when they were not dabbling in strictly political messages. In February 2017, he attacked Nordstrom after the department chain store decided to drop products associated with presidential daughter Ivanka Trump due to numerous calls for boycott.[1]

Even before assuming the office of president, the public personality that was Donald Trump viciously attacked corporations left and right, be it pharmaceutical companies, financial firms and others, and called for boycotts numerous times. The worst insults, however, both as private citizen and as president, he reserved for the media. As president, the same apparently vengeful and petty declarations have caused anger for the corporate backers of other Republican officials, thus in the officials themselves.

One victim of the president's attacks was Amazon, the flagship of Silicon Valley. The company is owned by Jeff Bezos, ranked as the richest man in history with a net worth of $150 billion. Bezos also owns *The Washington Post*, a longstanding critic of the president and his policies. While Amazon itself has not acted in a directly political fashion against Trump, it nevertheless attracted threats from the president, who argued that there was a possible antitrust case to be brought against the tech giant – threats which caused the stock price of Amazon to slightly drop.[2] Trump was voicing the same threats that he had used with AT&T and Time Warner – which owns his media nemesis, CNN – and

---

[1] Rachel Abrams, "Nordstrom drops Ivanka Trump brand from its stores," *The New York Times*, February 2nd, 2017, https://www.nytimes.com/2017/02/02/business/nordstrom-ivanka-trump.html.
[2] Michael D. Shear and Cecilia Kang, "Amazon has lots of company as Trump slams "stupid" businesses," *The New York Times*, April 3rd, 2018, https://www.nytimes.com/2018/04/03/us/politics/trump-amazon.html.

aircraft-manufacturer Boeing. The president considered all three corporate actors enemies, much like Nancy Pelosi or Alexandria Ocasio-Cortez.

Social media companies also came under the presidential gaze. Unlike most corporations, whose speech is manifested through ads and contributions, social media giants actually hold in their hands the modern-day public market in which opinions are shared and issues are discussed. Facebook, Twitter and their lesser competitors actually control speech, especially when not being on social media means not being seen or heard. This fact was understood by a United States federal district court judge who ruled in May, 2018, that President Donald Trump could not block people who disagreed with him from viewing his Twitter feed because it violated the First Amendment, thus making Twitter a "type of public forum in which the government may not, under the First Amendment, silence its critics."[3]

Evolving immensely since its conception, Facebook and its developers are having trouble coming to terms with the new reality, and rarely use their regulatory powers. In early March of 2018, however, Facebook removed a video posted by a member of the Hungarian government in which it stated that the "white Christians" of Hungary and Europe were threatened by minority communities. Posted ahead of the April elections in Hungary, the video was defended by Janos Lazar, minister of the prime minister's office of the same country. Lazar demanded that the video be reinstated and accused Facebook of infringing on his freedom of speech.[4] In the aftermath of the 2016 United States Presidential elections, however, social media platforms have been pressured to crack down on hate speech and misinformation, and they have responded by enforcing their own community standards. The notion that Facebook – a corporation nonetheless – is responsible for acting as watchdog of speech is readily accepted today, but would no doubt come as monstrous to the American forefathers.

Even small businesses have taken rather radical stances toward political issues and certain politicians. After consulting with her employees – who were asked to vote on the act – the owner of the Red Hen restaurant in Lexington, Virginia, asked White House press secretary Sarah Huckabee Sanders to leave the establishment. In doing so, she cited the establishment's values, "such as

---

[3] Josh Geltzer for Lydia Wheeler, "Judge Rules Trump Cannot Block Users on Twitter," *The Hill,* May 23rd, 2018, https://thehill.com/policy/technology/452160-appeals-court-rules-trump-cant-block-people-on-twitter.
[4] Lili Bayer, "Facebook removes Hungarian government video about 'white Christians,'" *Politico Europe,* March 7th 2018, https://www.politico.eu/article/white-christians-hungary-facebook-removent-government-video/.

honesty, and compassion and cooperation,"[5] or the fact that some of her employees were homosexual, and opposed them to the policy of separating families at the border, which secretary Sanders had defended, or the attacks of Vice-President Mike Pence against sexual minorities. In a revealing way, the owner did not mention her own values or opinions, but those upon which the restaurant was built and to which it was tied – values with which its employees and supposedly, even customers, identified.

In response to the Red Hen restaurant asking Sanders to leave, the president of the United States himself proceeded to attack the business – not the owner or the employees – saying it should "focus more on cleaning its filthy canopies, doors and windows."[6] Comments relating to a restaurant's cleanliness are obviously meant to discourage potential patrons from eating there, therefore potentially leading to bankruptcy, and that was exactly what president Trump aimed to do, to run the restaurant out of business for having the audacity of expressing a political stance. He did not criticize the owner of the restaurant, nor the employees for their voice – he went for the business, encouraging a boycott.

The Trump presidency has proven to be a transformative event regarding the involvement of corporations in the social life "of the city." While generally perceived as being "good for business" due to the corporate tax-cuts that he enacted, Trump also had a second effect on corporations. Divisive and always in the eye of a publicity storm, the 45th president of the United States and his scandalous acts also provided the context in which more and more artificial persons could express themselves through ads, campaign contributions, statements and acts in support of a certain cause. As every act for something is also an act against something, the corporations also stated the ideological ground on which they stood by these very acts.

Naturally, corporations are driven to act politically by other factors – the opinions and stances of their own managers and employees, the bouts of public opinion and perhaps most of all, the need to differentiate their otherwise interchangeable products from those of the competition, thus performing

---

[5] Bob Brigham, "Red Hen owner reveals she allowed employees to vote on booting Huckabee Sanders out of restaurant — and Sarah lost," *Raw Story*, June 23rd, 2018, https://www.rawstory.com/2018/06/red-hen-owner-reveals-allowed-employees-vote-booting-huckbee-sanders-restaurant-sarah-lost/.

[6] Mallory Shelbourne, "Trump: 'Dirty' restaurant that refused to serve Sanders 'needs a paint job'," *The Hill*, June 25th, 2018, https://thehill.com/homenews/administration/393900-trump-dirty-restaurant-that-refused-sanders-needs-a-paint-job.

"another bait and switch at the common good's expense"[7] while secretly aiming for high sales and hefty bonuses. In *The New York Times*, Douthat writes that corporations engage in political activism in such a public fashion because their managers and CEOs want to protect their own sphere of power from the progressive-originated criticism and policies. Thus, their whole act is meant to broker a "negotiated peace," to ensure that they "make money unmolested by the government."[8]

Except at that time, liberals and progressives were nowhere near positions of governmental or even legislative power. In 2018, business-friendly, tax-cutting and profit-cheering Republicans held the House of Representatives, the Senate and the Presidency. Douthat concedes the same fact, saying that this "peace" between progressives and corporations "won't be fully tested until the next time the Democrats hold real power."[9] Liberals had no governmental means through which to "molest" the supposedly money-hungry CEOs and managers of multinational corporations – unless public opinion and the existence of a viable alternative were involved.

While Douthat rightfully assumes that some corporations may be acting as the spearhead of progressive activism solely for profits, he entirely misses the scope of their action. Their newfound social role is not limited to influencing the government – specifically, a left-leaning government whose rise in taxes they seek to stop by preventively supporting some of their causes, such as minority rights. To the contrary, the Trump presidency has been a right-oriented one, focused on deregulation and the cutting of taxes. This is exactly why any friction that existed and will exist between the Trump government and corporations cannot be explained by the traditional political science literature, which remains blind to the changes brought about by corporate activism. Instead, the "college of corporations" responds to a society of consumers, who, split into ideological camps by the hyper-polarizing Trump presidency and more active and aware of the political environment than in the past decades, are far more likely to spend their disposable income and express a political opinion at the same time through, for example, buying Nike shoes in the aftermath of the Kaepernick campaign.

In August 2016, then-Republican presidential nominee Donald Trump posted a picture of himself eating from a KFC bucket on social media. Trump used KFC to make himself relatable, even though his failed ploy was immediately

---

[7] Ross Douthat, "The Rise of Woke Capital," *The New York Times*, February 28th, 2018, https://www.nytimes.com/2018/02/28/opinion/corporate-america-activism.html.
[8] Douthat, "The Rise of Woke Capital."
[9] Douthat, "The Rise of Woke Capital."

punished by critics.[10] Aside from that, a larger meaning can be ascribed to the attempt itself. The idea behind the system of democratic representation drawn up by the Founding Fathers of the United States – which served as a model to all subsequent democratic regimes – was that elected representatives are *representative*, that they come from the people and understand their lives, needs and desires. Instead, we have a candidate to the most important office in the United States reaching the people he seeks to represent through a corporation. It is the corporation that who interacts with American voters tens of millions of times per day, keeping in constant communication with them.

Who is to represent the people, politicians or corporations? Who is stronger, the voter or the consumer? In both cases, the latter seems to be the answer more and more, laying the path to a democratic system of the future that may bear little resemblance to the current one. But what about regimes that are anything but democratic? The EIU's 2020 Democracy Index notes that only half of the world's population lives in "full" or "flawed" democracies, the other half leading their lives under hybrid (15%) or authoritarian regimes (35.6%).[11] How are corporations to take charge of their political role as empowered persons and representatives of their consumers? The next chapter will attempt to answer the question by looking at how corporations have engaged in politics in the most important growing market – China.

---

[10] Adam Epstein, "'Regular guy' Donald Trump eats KFC with a knife and fork on his private jet," *Quartz*, August 2nd, 2016, https://qz.com/748241/regular-guy-donald-trump-eats-kfc-with-a-knife-and-fork-on-his-private-jet/.

[11] "Democracy Index 2020: In Sickness and in Health?" Pages.EIU.com, accessed January 16th 2021, https://pages.eiu.com/rs/753-RIQ-438/images/democracy-index-2020.pdf? mkt_tok=eyJpIjoiT0dFeU9USNOR1pppWlRneSIsInQiOiI0RmxteTd1K2xGN3hscFgzd1N WajY3RW9Bam84NmFteFVycDhxTkI0WjVXM0dsOFBXdzlQajVPYXFmemRUcEJyQjlsSH VibVwvc2dQeHBBQzlRT0RncFZCZCU1Y5NXNwYWtRMnBSZklOVVhIaG84Q2F0cjhzcnlya mNUNUxzdUJuY0cifQ%3D%3D.

Chapter XII

China vs. Corporations

North America and Europe are not the only places in which corporations have had to engage in political and social debates, sometimes entirely without their intention. In China, identified by the EIU as clearly authoritarian, corporations such as Mercedes-Benz, Marriot, Apple, McDonald's, Versace and others have seen themselves thrown against the political grinding machine that is the Communist Party. Founded in 1921 and undemocratically ruling the country since 1949, the Communist Party has overseen grand projects of development that resulted in countless deaths. To this day, the one party is reportedly making use of forced labor – particularly that of the Muslim Uighur population that is imprisoned in work camps and treated as slaves.[1] The state-centered, totalitarian power system, the unfair justice system and the state-owned giant enterprises make China one of the most unlikely environments in which Western corporations could operate. At the same time, however, the economic growth of China is undeniable. In 2000, the World Bank put China's GDP at $1.2 billion, but in 2018 it jumped to $13.6 billion. The country is also home to a fifth of the world population, almost 1.4 billion potential consumers with a life expectancy that has grown by 6 years over the last two decades.[2] For companies all over the globe, China is a virtual gold rush, a market that cannot be ignored. Asia as a whole "was the largest recipient of capital inflows prior to 1997, accounting for almost 50% of total flows to all developing countries in the first half of the decade."[3] However, it was China that emerged as the leading recipient of foreign direct investments (FDI) in the developing world. The result was quick to be seen. The number of Chinese people living in extreme poverty fell from 53% in 1981 to 1.9% in 2017.[4] That translates into hundreds of millions of new consumers every decade. Although FDI from developed democracies

---

[1] Adrian Zenz, "Xinjiang's New Slavery," *Foreign Policy*, December 11th, 2019, https://foreignpolicy.com/2019/12/11/cotton-china-uighur-labor-xinjiang-new-slavery/.

[2] "Country Data – China," WorldBank.org, accessed December 30th 2019, https://data.worldbank.org/country/china.

[3] Thomas Oatley, *International Political Economy* (New York & London: Routledge, 2019), 430.

[4] Oatley, 208.

can generally exert "a significant positive effect on democracy"[5] in the recipient economies, a lot of factors come into play, such as the sector of investments and the distribution of FDI. While countries like China highlight market-supporting institutions and an iron-clad level of domestic stability[6] to attract FDI, mainly through bilateral investment treaties, the fact remains that corporations that invest in authoritarian countries place their money at the whims of an unaccountable government whose demise – although distant at the moment – may be explosive. Even the endurance of such a government may also prove dangerous as changes of heart, due to changes in leadership or priorities, can endanger said investments.

Such dangers existed even before corporations became political actors. The new reality adds another layer to the relationship between authoritarian governments and corporations. China, however, is in a special position. As the purchasing power of the individual Chinese keeps growing, so does the power that the government has over multinational corporations, for it controls the access to the consumer base, and does not have to answer in front of its people at the polls. Conversely, wherever consumers are poor, authoritarian governments depend on the FDI that accompany multinational corporations to satisfy their people – and so are unlikely to criticize them.

But China is special. If in the Western democratic world consumers can individually choose which corporation to support with their newly fashioned vote – i.e. the shopping cart –, in China they have no such freedom, just as they cannot choose their leaders. Economic freedom and political freedom have become one, and China exemplifies the new reality. The Communist government of the country can deny access to the consumers, essentially becoming itself the sole, giant consumer voice that needs pleasing, the only one whose values matter. An affront to the Party amounts to an affront to the entire consumer mass of the country, as there is no opposing mass of consumers to balance its force, the same way there is no opposing political force to the Communist Party. For corporations, China is a Party with a market, and getting to the latter entails obtaining the permission of the former.

Although the most visible through its size, the Chinese case is not singular. As a whole, FDI inflows to Asia grew from $70.2 billion in 1990-1999 to $440.8

---

[5] Feng Sun, "The Dual Political Effects of Foreign Direct Investment in Developing Countries," *The Journal of Developing Areas* 48, 1 (Winter 2014): pp. 107-125 https://doi.org/10.1353/jda.2014.0020.
[6] Lin Cui and Chungshik Moon, "What Attracts Foreign Direct Investment Into Autocratic States? Regime Time Horizon and Institutional Design," *The World Economy* 43, 10 (April 2020): pp. 2762-2784 https://doi.org/10.1111/twec.12956.

billion between 2010 and 2016.[7] The FDI inflows serve to fill in the gaps of missing information, signaling where international corporations choose to direct their presence, and therefore their money. Acting outside the world of consolidated democracies is therefore something that corporations have to do to thrive and grow.

Appeasing the Chinese government, then, becomes essential for any corporation that wishes to access the golden market. Corporations operating in China cannot act as representatives, they cannot be progressive or conservative in their values because the sole consumer voice incentivizing them is that of the ruling Communist Party. There is no political plurality in China that corporations could represent. Missing the key developmental stage of being a democracy – much less a liberal democracy –, China cannot evolve into a corporate-led democracy.

As such, in China corporations are aggressively and routinely reduced to their inferior state of purely economic agents whenever the government feels that its authority has been challenged or that its pride has been insulted. Even so, the fact that a supposedly economic agent can bring harm to the reputation of a totalitarian party brings into question whether or not that agent is entirely without political significance. This has led to several situations such as the one in February of 2018, when a car manufacturer and one of the most well-known auto brands, Mercedes-Benz, apologized to the "Chinese people" after quoting the Dalai Lama in one of its Instagram posts. The quote, accompanying a white Mercedes car, simply stated "look at the situations from all angles, and you will become more open." However, the Tibetan spiritual leader is considered to be a dangerous rebel and separatist by the Chinese authorities, which have exiled him from the country. Mercedes' post, therefore, showed support to a rebel in the eyes of the Chinese government. After deleting the post, Mercedes issued apologies and promised to "take steps to deepen our understanding of Chinese culture and values."[8]

Another international corporation that had to apologize to the Chinese government was the hotel chain Marriott. In January 2018, Marriott issued an online customer questionnaire that listed Tibet, Taiwan, Hong Kong and Macau as separate from China. Tibet has been a part of China since 1950, Hong Kong and Macau were returned to the Chinese government in the 1990s but Taiwan maintains its independence, despite contestation from Beijing. As a reply, the

---

[7] Cui and Moon, ""What Attracts Foreign Direct Investment Into Autocratic States?" 227.

[8] Pei Li and Adam Jourdan, "Mercedes-Benz apologizes to Chinese for quoting Dalai Lama," *Business Insider*, February 6th, 2018, https://www.reuters.com/article/us-mercedes-benz-china-gaffe/mercedes-benz-apologizes-to-chinese-for-quoting-dalai-lama-idUSKBN1FQ1FJ.

country's internet watchdog, the Cyberspace Administration, closed Marriott's website and booking applications for a week, effectively instituting a total boycott against the 100 Marriott hotels in China. The punishment came with a motivation – Marriott had "hurt the feelings of the Chinese people" and violated Chinese laws. As China is Marriott's biggest market,[9] the hotel chain quickly issued an apology and made its stance on separatist movements clear, saying "we don't support separatist groups that subvert the sovereignty and territorial integrity of China."[10] After the statement, numerous online commentators[11] argued that Marriott should be boycotted in turn for appeasing the Chinese authorities who routinely imprison supporters of greater regional autonomy for the abovementioned regions.

Clothing retailer Gap, which has around 300 stores in Asia, also had its own run-in with the enraged Chinese authorities after displaying a shirt with a map of China that did not include Taiwan, Tibet and the islands in the South China Sea that Beijing claims as its own. Pictures of the shirt circulated on the microblogging site Weibo, popular in China, and became viral. Hours later, Gap issued a statement in which it apologized for the "unintentional mistake" and argued that it completely "respects the sovereignty and territorial integrity of China."[12] The retailer also stated that the product was pulled from the shelves and destroyed. Even unintentionally, Gap showed that corporations can act as very visible critics of territorial disputes between countries. With a mere shirt, Gap managed to speak volumes.

In the summer of 2019, Versace had a similar experience as Gap. It managed to infuriate the Chinese government with another shirt that had the same message as the one marketed by the Gap – only this time without a map.[13] The Versace shirt, which lists countries and capitals, appeared to say that Hong Kong and Macau are independent countries, city-states that had no connection to China, even though they are technically part of it despite their greater degree of autonomy as regions. Just as Gap, Versace issued an apology and destroyed

---

[9] Benjamin Haas, "Marriott apologises to China over Tibet and Taiwan error," *The Guardian*, January 12th, 2018, https://www.theguardian.com/world/2018/jan/12/marriott-apologises-to-china-over-tibet-and-taiwan-error.

[10] "China shuts Marriott's website over Tibet and Taiwan error," *BBC*, January 12th, 2018, https://www.bbc.com/news/business-42658070.

[11] "China shuts Marriott's website."

[12] Tiffany Hsu, "Gap, Wary of Crossing China, Apologizes for T-Shirt's Map," *The New York Times*, May 15th 2018, https://www.nytimes.com/2018/05/15/business/gap-china-apology.html.

[13] Nikhil Sonnad, "Versace is the latest major brand to express its 'deepest apologies' to China," *Quartz*, August 11th, 2019, https://qz.com/1685587/versace-the-latest-brand-to-express-deepest-apologies-to-china/.

all of the shirts that it had not sold. Writing for *Quartz*, Sonnad notes that the same "mistake," namely that of appearing to consider Taiwan, China and Hong Kong as being different countries, was also committed by Delta, Zara and McDonald's – and all had to issue apologies.[14]

If corporations in the United States and Europe see themselves dragged into debates and controversies regarding racism, immigration, climate change and sexism, in China they are accidentally actors in territorial disputes. The major difference is that in the Western world corporations are most often in dialogue with consumers or *consumer activists* who seek to influence them and their policies or influence officials through the corporations. In this way, the new voter, the consumer, is exercising the power of the corporation, its new representative. In China, on the other hand, the sole partner of dialogue for the corporations is the Chinese government, which considers itself the only voice of the people in any capacity. If the shopping cart is the new vote, then China's government holds all Chinese votes, nullifying any representative duty from the part of the corporations.

The strained relationship between international corporations and the Communist government of China was made more apparent by the wave of protests that overcame Hong Kong. In April of 2019, an extradition bill allowing criminal suspects to be taken from the island of Hong Kong to mainland China was introduced in Hong Kong's legislature. Critics of the bill immediately pointed out that such a bill would expose the citizens of Hong Kong, who live under a different system than the Chinese, to unfair trials and the violence of a regime that still operates work camps.

The people of Hong Kong took to the streets and violent clashes with the police ensued even after the bill was withdrawn, dragging out the conflict for months.[15] The prolonged protest received much attention from international media, even though action from the part of the liberal democratic governments of the world was lacking. Corporations were caught in the crossfire of the two sides as well, between a Western consumer base that was sympathetic to the plight of the protesters and a Chinese government that controlled the access to the world's largest market of consumers.

In Hong Kong, itself a bastion of business in Asia, the protesters targeted not only government buildings, but also Chinese businesses, banks and pro-Beijing corporations. Chatterjee and Roantree note for Reuters that the outlets of the Bank of China were trashed – but that those of the international Standard Chartered bank were untouched. Protesters threatened that they "will target all

---

[14] Sonnad, "Versace."
[15] As this book is being written, the protests are still ongoing.

the pro-China business groups who don't *speak* out against [China's efforts to restrict freedom]."[16] Chinese tech giant Xiaomi also had its Hong Kong offices attacked. Starbucks coffee shops, which are operated in Hong Kong by a local company named Maxim's Caterers, were also targeted after the daughter of the founder of Maxim's publicly condemned the protesters.[17]

The corporations present in Hong Kong were asked to *speak* in defense of the pro-democracy protesters in Hong Kong and those who were associated with China through their identity – Bank of China, Xiaomi – as well as those who stood with China willingly, were punished. Such acts make no sense if those in question are purely economic agents operating on the basis of strict demand and supply, with no political dimension.

Corporations were involved in the Hong Kong protests not only through their physical presence on the island, but also directly through their products. In October, Chinese state media *The People's Daily* accused the American tech corporation Apple of no less than protecting the protesters through its app HKmap.live which tracked the movements of the Chinese police in the city. The app, which Apple first rejected then approved and integrated in its App Store, was aggregating inputs from Hong Kongers all over the island in order to pinpoint the exact location of the police forces, allowing the pro-democracy protestors to be one step ahead and avoid capture. Through its state-controlled media outlets, the Chinese government asked "has Apple thought clearly about this?"[18] The Communist government was not accusing foreign intervention in its internal political affairs by another government or governmental agency, but by a tech corporation that was *equipping* its opponents with technology. *The People's Daily* piece went on, condemning Apple's "*mixing of political, commercial* and illegal activities."[19]

Soon after, however, Apple went back on its decision a third time and removed the same app in what critics dubbed as a bow to the Chinese government. Writing for *Gizmondo* in criticism of the decision, Novak notes that it was not the first time that Apple appeased the Communist government

---

[16] Sumeet Chatterjee and Anne Marie Roantree, "Mainland banks, pro-Beijing businesses caught in Hong Kong protest cross-hairs," *Reuters*, October 2nd, 2019, https://www.reuters.com/article/us-hongkong-protests-cleanup/mainland-banks-pro-beijing-businesses-caught-in-hong-kong-protest-cross-hairs-idUSKBN1WH055.
[17] "Why Starbucks? The brands being attacked in Hong Kong," *BBC*, October 11th, 2019, https://www.bbc.com/news/world-asia-china-49983767.
[18] Verna Yu, "'Protecting rioters': China warns Apple over app that tracks Hong Kong police," *The Guardian*, October 9th, 2019, https://www.theguardian.com/world/2019/oct/09/protecting-rioters-china-warns-apple-over-app-that-tracks-hong-kong-police.
[19] Yu, "'Protecting rioters'."

– the company had also banned hundreds of VPNs, which amounted to censoring users, removed the Taiwan flag emoji, and banned the QZ news app. Just as other corporations before it, Apple was protecting its access to what had become its largest market after the United States.[20] The company's defense, however, was as political as it could have been. Tim Cook, CEO of Apple, wrote to all Apple employees in the aftermath of the corporation's removal of HKmap.live, arguing that "technology can be used for good or for ill. [...] Over the past several days we received credible information, from the Hong Kong Cybersecurity and Technology Crime Bureau, as well as from users in Hong Kong, that the app was being used maliciously to target individual officers for violence and to victimize individuals and property where no police are present."[21]

Another corporation that gave in to Beijing's pressures in the context of the Hong Kong protests was sneaker retailer Vans. In the autumn of 2019, the company held its annual Custom Culture shoe contest, inviting artists and designers to pitch their own style of sneakers. An artist based in Canada submitted a sneaker that featured the Hong Kong protestors, their yellow umbrellas and the flag of Hong Kong on the side of the shoe. The entry received the majority of the votes of the audience and was poised to earn the cash prize. Also as a prize, Vans had promised to produce the sneakers.[22] Before the competition ended, however, the company decided to withdraw the proposed design, prompting Hong Kongers to go on social media and post videos of themselves *throwing or burning their Vans sneakers away* while using the hashtag #boycottVans. Vans was receiving the same treatment that Nike had, except the latter was being boycotted by conservatives in the United States, whereas Vans had enraged pro-democracy Hong Kongers. Interestingly, in June of the same year, Nike had to pull a series of products from its stores in China out of fear for pushback from the Chinese government. The brand was selling sneakers in the region in partnership with the Japanese streetwear label Undercover – and Undercover had posted a picture on its Instagram account earlier that month in support of the Hong Kong protesters, writing "no

---

[20] Vlad Savov and Mark Gurman, "Apple Pulls App That Tracks Police Activity in Hong Kong," *Bloomberg*, October 10th, 2019, https://www.bloomberg.com/news/articles/2019-10-10/apple-reverses-course-again-bans-controversial-hong-kong-app.

[21] Alex Hern, "Tim Cook defends Apple's removal of Hong Kong mapping app," *The Guardian*, October 10th, 2019, https://www.theguardian.com/technology/2019/oct/10/tim-cook-apple-hong-kong-mapping-app-removal.

[22] Zoe Suen, "Vans Competition Pulls Sneaker Brand Into Hong Kong Political Row," *Business of Fashion*, October 4th, 2019, https://www.businessoffashion.com/articles/news-analysis/vans-competition-pulls-sneaker-brand-into-hong-kong-political-row.

extradition to China" and "go Hong Kong."[23] A progressive actor willing to take bold stances in the United States, Nike was more cautious in China.

Defending its decision with regard to the sneaker design contest, Vans released a statement saying "we have never taken a political position and therefore review designs to ensure they are in line with our company's long-held values of respect and tolerance."[24] The corporation was attempting to de-politicize its products, but by censoring the artist's design it had already *spoken* – and it had spoken against the protests.

In China, then, corporations are not representatives of their consumers. They do not speak for or against certain divisive, political measures or issues, and they do not intentionally challenge the government. Their run-ins with the Chinese government, however, still showcase the power of corporate speech. Following Oatley, approaching corporations on the international stage should be an economic, cut-and-dry topic. A traditional way to summarize the traditional approach would be to argue that

> The politics of MNCs emerge from the competing interests of host countries, home countries of the MNCs, and the MNCs themselves. Each group has distinctive interests regarding FDI. MNCs want to operate freely across the globe, with few government-imposed restrictions on their activities. Host countries want to ensure that the MNCs operating within their borders provide benefits to the local economy that offset the loss of decision-making authority that is inherent in foreign ownership. The home countries of the MNCs want to ensure that their firms' overseas investments are secure. The politics of MNCs emerge when these distinct interests come into conflict with each other.[25]

In China, all three interests identified above are serviced. China prospers from foreign, corporate FDIs, the corporations themselves turn a profit, and home countries have the knowledge that their firms' investments are safe. Still, as shown above, the Chinese government, wielding uncontested political power as the sole representative of the Chinese people, repeatedly felt

---

[23] Michelle Toh and Laura He, "Nike pulls products in China after designer sparks social media outrage," *CNN*, June 27th, 2019, https://edition.cnn.com/2019/06/27/business/nike-china-japan-hong-kong/index.html.

[24] Jessie Yeung, "Vans faces Hong Kong boycott over sneaker design controversy," *CNN*, October 7th, 2019, https://edition.cnn.com/style/article/vans-hong-kong-intl-hnk-scli/index.html.

[25] Thomas Oatley, *International Political Economy*, p. 276.

challenged by corporations. It only follows that the latter are not mere economic agents and that the Gap can speak through a shirt just as well – or more powerfully – than an NGO or a foreign official, and certainly more resoundingly than any individual, natural person. As corporations spread across the globe more and more, operating outside democratic traditions and norms of political plurality and freedom of speech, clashes between them and authoritarian regimes are more and more likely to occur. While the Chinese government spoke to corporations from a position of power, as the unelected but uncontested guardian of a massive, newly-rich consumer base, not all undemocratic governments will be able to do the same. Some, stewarding poor economies thirsty for FDI, will have to accept the Gap's shirt, or Vans' contest. In the new world, then, the main contesters of dictators, juntas and single parties could be corporations.

Conclusion

The Chinese episode in the saga of corporations shows that *corporate-led democracy*, the political and social system in which corporations are the main movers and shakers, the representatives of their actual and potential consumers and the voice through which these address the state – which can, by now, be described as an apparatus of governing disconnected from everyday individuals and driven solely by inertia – cannot come to be if it is not preceded by a consolidated liberal democratic system. No corporate representation of consumer values can occur under regimes that do not permit meaningful, democratic representation and the voicing of criticism toward the governing bodies to begin with. These authoritarian bodies can and will, by definition, impose certain values and therefore make any debate and any representation redundant.

But China is also an exception in the globalized and interconnected economic and, as this book argues, political market, as the central government there holds the access key to the world's fastest-growing market, to over a billion consumers that have increasingly more disposable income at hand, and thus occupies an advantageous position in relation to any corporation. By comparison, an equally oppressive government overseeing a poor country would hold little sway over international corporations, if any had an interest in the respective country to begin with – which is not very likely. The fact that one of Gap's shirts is somehow offensive to North Korea is not likely to lead to the extraction of an apology for the simple fact that North Koreans are not consumers of the Gap's products. China's relationship with corporations, then, cannot be generalized to other authoritarian regimes – rather, it is the reverse of the situation in the United States, where corporations are recognized as political actors enjoying the rights any person does within a consolidated liberal democracy.

Corporate democracy must necessarily appear out of the disillusioned masses which have lost interest in political parties, which distrust state institutions and that cannot find it within themselves to cast a vote or be active in any meaningful and traditional political manner anymore, despite any promise. It must appear out of the grave of the voter as the system which empowers the consumer and makes him the source of the directives by which corporations orient themselves and their new political power and in turn shape the state. The political protests of the future will not occur in front of the US Congress or the White House, but in front of the Coca-Cola headquarters in Atlanta, or the Amazon offices in Seattle – and these corporations will have to listen, for if they do not, then PepsiCo, Keurig Dr. Pepper, or Alibaba and Walmart will.

For the same reason, corporate-led democracy will not affect corporations who hold virtual monopolies over a consumer base, as they may have no incentive to represent the values of said consumers due to the lack of competition. Not unlike the situation in which a political party holds an electorate captive or monopolizes all political power, such a corporation sees no threat to its consumer-provided revenue stream and faces no challenge from the part of a market competitor, being therefore free to ignore any consumer values. The captor does not ask of the desires of the captives, and this applies to both one-party political systems and monopolistic economic relations.

The present book has shown that despite their wealth and their ability to pour endless resources into any political campaign, corporations do not extract their power from influencing decision-makers and state officials. They do so by being recognizable to every individual, child or adult, by being the recipients of millions of inputs every day through their role as providers of goods and services. Who better knows what one's weekly shopping cart holds and how rising prices will hurt that person, a socialist party or Wal-Mart?

The great mistake that critics of politically-involved corporation make is that they do not understand that the corporate influencing of politicians happens only after the consumers have provided their inputs to the corporation through their interaction – with their purchases. It is only to satisfy them – and yes, profit – that the corporation becomes involved with sensible political and social issues.

When fascism broke out in Italy and later took power, in 1922, the Third Communist International, taking place at the same time, labeled it as the latest manifestation of corporate interests acting in the corrupt system that was capitalism, noting in its proceedings that "everywhere capitalism relies not just on its organs of state power but on other, special bodies to defend its property and to oppress and disperse the working class."[1] According to them, Mussolini's black shirts were the avatar under which companies and industrial groups finally decided to control society directly, and not through the intermediaries that were the democratic and liberal politicians and parties. From that moment on, as the label was hardly under any debate within the communist groups themselves, the concept of businesses, especially large industries, as being fascist took hold over left-leaning intellectuals and movements across the

[1] "Session 15," in *To the masses: Proceedings of the Third Congress of the Communist International*, ed. John Riddell (Leiden & Bristol: Brill, 1921), p. 624.

world, even after the Second World War. Coupled with the myth that Mussolini and Hitler were aided by businessmen throughout their ascension and during their time in power – which was later disproved[2] – the idea that corporations were inherently conservative, right-wing and fascistic always struck the right cord with the anti-capitalists.

But the contemporary reality undoubtedly disproves such a thesis.

The largest international corporations of today have proven to be increasingly progressive. From Nike to Coca-Cola, Target and Tiffany's, they have recognized and stood up for same-sex marriage, the right to protest, LGBT rights, transparency, the rights of migrants, abortion, social responsibility, environmentalism and much more. Corporations and their political influence, overcoming national boundaries and regulations due to their economic reach and sheer size, would perhaps greatly temper nationalist tendencies – for they have to sell their products outside of their home country. What is more, corporations have no ethnicity and no religious faith. Instead of a monolithic state led by ethnocratic parties and leaders, preferring a diminished form of political and economic autarky, we would have clusters of influence and political potency, primarily ensured by financial capital, that would necessarily be wedded to the values and wishes of consumers, and as corporations seek to expand their consumer base, a centripetal force would always be at work, much stronger than in the case of the median voter.

Following the Protestant work ethic,[3] the men and women composing the feared, sometimes hated multinational corporations already possess a claim to public office and decision, simply due to their economic status, which undoubtedly signals competence. Is a successful background in the private sector not an advantage when standing for public office in any liberal democracy? As majoritarianism – as a system of thought – gets stronger and stronger, especially with the rise of populist movements, a society governed by responsible corporations, committed to political pluralism due to their inherent acceptance of economic pluralism, becomes more viable, representing a check on the manipulative media of "post-truth" and the passionate, unreasonable electorate. The same Nike, Coca-Cola, Target and others cannot afford to be anti-Semitic or homophobic, as their profits come from Jewish and non-heterosexual consumers as well as any other group of potential clients. Due to their origins as economic agents whose *raison d'être* is to amass profits by appealing to as large a consumer base as possible, the

---

[2] Jonah Goldberg, *Liberal Fascism: The Secret History of the American Left, From Mussolini to the Politics of Change* (London: Random House, 2009).

[3] Max Weber, *The Protestant Ethic and the Spirit of Capitalism* (London: Routledge, 2001).

politically-empowered corporations can hardly afford to even be seen as intolerant to any group.

It is, indeed, a "brave new world," one in which corporations will increasingly carry more political weight – more than they already do – not only because of their economic resources. The *Citizens United* ruling, although essential, comes only as a confirmation of a larger trend. This phenomenon can be observed in the cradle of modern liberal democracy and the most successful model of the functioning of market economy – the United States of America. However, the implications of the *Citizens United* ruling have not yet been interiorized neither by the politicians, nor by the corporations themselves. The present trend, proven by public data concerning campaign financing in the United States and by the numerous episodes presented above, confirms the book's hypothesis – that the time of "natural" persons is dawning, while that of "artificial persons" is only beginning.

The reconceptualization of the corporation and its incorporation into the mainstream political science literature as an actor is inevitable. To not do so is to refuse evidence that is strengthened day after day and to confine politics, not to mention scholarly research, into a cave populated solely by shadows that offer no explanation of their own nature or that of their acts. To prevent such a state, future research will necessarily revolve around a string of key questions – what is the threshold above which a corporation is driven to involve itself into political and social debates ongoing in the larger society? Why does Nike do it, but not fellow makers of sneakers Fila or Reebok? Why are progressive consumers dominant – or at least more vocal and organized – in the US market? What is the most effective way to transform and incentivize a corporation into adopting a certain set of values? The questions abound and the answers are painfully lacking, a situation that needs immediate attention from the part of the political science departments across the world.

Democracy is indeed in crisis, a fashionable statement in political science ever since Samuel P. Huntington, Joji Watanuki and Michel Crozier put it into words in 1975,[4] but not because the membership percentages in established democracies are decreasing, nor because populist parties defined by intolerance and hatred are on the rise. Democracy is in crisis because it is forcing itself to ignore its strongest political players, the corporations, and their capacity to innovate a political area voided of dynamic relations.

---

[4] Michel Crozier, Samuel P. Huntington, Joji Watanuki, *The Crisis of Democracy: Report on the Governability of Democracies to the Trilateral Commission* (New York: New York University Press, 1975).

Smaller and necessarily efficient in their organization, corporations have often been one step ahead of the governments and parliaments of the world. In 2004, Ireland introduced a total smoking ban and backed it up with a hefty fine of 3.000 euros. With the benefit of hindsight, one can say that the measure was a long time coming, seeing as the first medical reports detailing the adverse effects of smoking were available starting from 1964.[5] Still, Ireland was the first country in the world to do so. McDonald's, however, did it in 1994, a full decade earlier.[6] The largest fast-food chain back then as well, McDonald's went smoke-free in all of its US restaurants that year. Moreover, along with Burger King, Wendy's, Taco Bell and other names in the fast-food industry, McDonald's decided to back federal anti-smoking legislation. In response, the tobacco industry at that time warned the fast-food industry that it may lose customers as a result of this smoking ban[7] – which amounted to a veiled threat of boycotts.

Unseen or misinterpreted, the new reality of the corporate democracy was already forming, and McDonald's was already a better representative of public opinion in 1994 than elected officials all over the democratic world.

As this book has shown, the newly empowered companies, the Corporate Overlords, will necessarily submit to a power higher than them – the consumer. Liberal democracy centers on the will of the citizen and even the most minimalist definition of democracy includes voting. That will still be the case in corporate democracy as well, except the voter will cede his place to the consumer. It is the consumer who will drive the political leanings of a company and the extent to which they will be activist. It is the consumer, and not the voter, who will decide what words can be used and in what context, which type of discourse is acceptable and which is not, how companies will react to policies and where donations will go. For all their power, the overlords will conduct themselves out of an existential need to represent a wider part as possible of the consumer base. This drive comes out of the need of corporations to have as many sales as possible in order to increase revenue, but it will temper their political activism – and that of the consumers and the politicians they interact with.

---

[5] Institute of Medicine (US) Committee on Secondhand Smoke Exposure and Acute Coronary Events. *Secondhand Smoke Exposure and Cardiovascular Effects: Making Sense of the Evidence.* Washington (DC): National Academies Press (US); 2010.
[6] Kristin Downey Grimsley, "McDonald's restaurants going smoke-free," *The Washington Post*, February 24th, 1994, https://www.washingtonpost.com/archive/politics/1994/02/24/mcdonalds-restaurants-going-smoke-free/a308b6e6-53b4-4451-b364-5c10739ab723/.
[7] Grimsley, "McDonald's."

Corporations are stronger citizens, as their voices are louder. They are effective regulators, as they can, for example, silence someone by simply de-platforming them. In many ways, they regulate access to resources and services.[8] They are also more responsive representatives, as their need for profit makes them especially attentive to the wants of the consumers.

In the past, corporations have been associated with fascism, due to misunderstood theory that employed the same word – corporatism – and blamed for all the ills of the world, most of all due to greed. But it is their supposed greed that can make them greener, more responsible, more engaged, more social, more just, more representative. The newly-gained place of corporations in democracy will impact the system in its entirety.

A day will come in the not-so-distant future when an individual will prefer his mantle of a consumer to that of the voter when he will address Google, Nike and Wal-Mart to advance gender equality, gun rights or climate action, and not the Republican, Democratic or any other political party, much less the state institutions.

> As corporations speak, all will listen.
> But they will be speaking with our voice.

---

[8] In early 2021, the Democratic governor of Nevada, Steve Sisolak, promoted a plan to create "Innovation Zones." These were autonomous, corporate-ran local governments that could, among others, impose taxes. The drafted piece of legislation in question described "traditional" local government models as "inadequate" to emerging technologies and proposed the creation of an "alternative form of local government," namely government by corporations. Blockchains LLC, a tech firm that gave money to both Democrats and Republicans though PACs, took up Sisolak's offer and bought 67,000 acres of undeveloped, uninhabited land. Colton Lochhead, "Bill would allow tech companies to create local governments," *Las Vegas Review-Journal*, February 3rd, 2021, https://www.reviewjournal.com/news/politics-and-government/2021-legislature/bill-would-allow-tech-companies-to-create-local-governments-2272887/.

Bibliography

Abrams, Rachel. "Nordstrom drops Ivanka Trump brand from its stores," *The New York Times*, February 2nd, 2017, https://www.nytimes.com/2017/02/02/business/nordstrom-ivanka-trump.html.

Airbnb Press Room. "Listings in Disputed Regions." Airbnb.com. (Accessed December 3rd 2018) https://news.airbnb.com/listings-in-disputed-regions/.

Amatulli, Jenna. "Johnnie Walker releases 'Jane Walker' to celebrate women's rights," *Huffington Post*, February 27th, 2018, https://www.huffpost.com/entry/johnnie-walker-releases-jane-walker-whiskey-to-celebrate-womens-rights_n_5a957944e4b0bef79e3045ba.

Anapol, Avery. "Gillette takes on toxic masculinity in new ad campaign," *The Hill*, January 14th, 2019, https://thehill.com/blogs/blog-briefing-room/news/425190-gillette-takes-on-toxic-masculinity-in-new-ad-campaign.

Andrews, Travis. "The President Stole Your Land': Patagonia, REI Blast Trump On National Monument Rollbacks," *The Washington Post*, December 5th, 2017, https://www.washingtonpost.com/news/morning-mix/wp/2017/12/05/the-president-stole-your-land-patagonia-rei-blast-trump-on-national-monument-rollbacks/.

AP News. "Netflix will 'rethink' Georgia shoots if abortion law holds," May 28th, 2019, https://apnews.com/82bc083f3131474b9643ac870b30010b.

Batha, Emma. "Pink for girls: does toy marketing affect girls' career choices?" *Reuters*, April 30th, 2019, https://www.reuters.com/article/us-britain-children-marketing/pink-for-girls-does-toy-marketing-affect-girls-career-choices-idUSKCN1S52AD.

Bayer, Lili. "Facebook removes Hungarian government video about 'white Christians'," *Politico Europe*, March 7th, 2018, https://www.politico.eu/article/white-christians-hungary-facebook-removent-government-video/.

BBC. "China shuts Marriott's website over Tibet and Taiwan error," January 12th, 2018, https://www.bbc.com/news/business-42658070.

BBC. "Georgia abortion: WarnerMedia joins Disney and Netflix in considering options," May 30th, 2019, https://www.bbc.com/news/entertainment-arts-48457401.

BBC. "Iranian hardliners threaten taxi app boycott in hijab row," June 11th, 2019, https://www.bbc.com/news/blogs-trending-48593981.

BBC. "Why Starbucks? The brands being attacked in Hong Kong," October 11th, 2019, https://www.bbc.com/news/world-asia-china-49983767.

Bhattarai, Abha. "Amazon is seeking a home for HQ2, a $5 billion second headquarters somewhere in North America," *Washington Post*, September 8th, 2017, https://www.washingtonpost.com/news/business/wp/2017/09/07/amazon-is-looking-for-a-city-to-site-a-second-5-billion-headquarters/.

Bliss, Laura. "Lyft will offer free rides to anti-gun rallies," *CityLab*, March 2nd, 2018, https://www.citylab.com/transportation/2018/03/lyft-will-offer-free-rides-to-anti-gun-rallies/554756/.

Blume, K. Allan. "'Guilty as charged,' Cathy says of Chick-fil-A's stand on biblical & family values," *Baptist Press*, July 16th, 2012, http://www.bpnews.net/38271/guilty-as-charged-cathy-says-of-chickfilas-stand-on-biblical-and -family-values.

Bomey, Nathan. "Wal-Mart bans gun sales to anyone under 21 after Parkland, Florida school shooting," *USA Today*, March 1st, 2018, https://eu.usatoday.com/story/money/2018/02/28/walmart-bans-gun-sales-anyone-under-21-after-parkland-florida-school-shooting/383487002/.

Bosa, Deirdre. "Lyft claims it now has more than one-third of the US ride-sharing market," *CNBC*, March 14th, 2018, https://www.cnbc.com/2018/05/14/lyft-market-share-051418-bosa-sf.html.

Bowden, John. "Twitter CEO Jack Dorsey: I 'fully admit' our bias is 'more left-leaning'," *The Hill*, August 18th, 2018, https://thehill.com/policy/technology/402495-twitter-ceo-jack-dorsey-i-fully-admit-our-bias-is-more-left-leaning.

Brenan, Megan. "Record-Low 46% of Women Pleased with Society's Treatment," *Gallup News*, March 16th, 2019, https://news.gallup.com/poll/246056/record-low-women-pleased-society-treatment.aspx.

Brigham, Bob. "Red Hen owner reveals she allowed employees to vote on booting Huckabee Sanders out of restaurant — and Sarah lost," *Raw Story*, June 23rd, 2018, https://www.rawstory.com/2018/06/red-hen-owner-reveals-allowed-employees-vote-booting-huckbee-sanders-restaurant-sarah-lost/.

Bruenig, Elizabeth. "Laura Ingraham's advertisers aren't really staging a boycott. It's a capital strike," *The Washington Post*, April 4th, 2018, https://www.washingtonpost.com/opinions/laura-ingrahams-advertisers-arent-really-staging-a-boycott-its-a-capital-strike/2018/04/04/aba91dd2-382a-11e8-acd5-35eac230e514_story.html.

Canfield, George. "The Scope and Limits of the Corporate Entity Theory." *Columbia Law Review* 17, 2 (February 1917): pp. 128-143.

Carlson, Tucker, "Tucker Carlson: Big Business Hates Your Family - National Conservatism Conference," YouTube video, 53:37 minutes, July 18th 2019, https://www.youtube.com/watch?v=AXGoWtK1NnY&ab_channel=National Conservatism.

Carrig, David. "KFC replaces iconic Colonel Sanders with his wife to honor International Women's Day in Malaysia," *USA Today*, March 8th, 2018, https://eu.usatoday.com/story/money/business/2018/03/08/kfc-replaces-iconic-col-sanders-international-womens-day/406308002/.

Center for Responsive Politics. "Super PACs: How Many Donors Give." OpenSecrets.org. (Accessed on March 15th 2019). https://www.opensecrets.org/outside-spending/donor-stats.

Cerullo, Megan. "Peloton ad costs the company and shareholders $1.6 billion," *CBS News*, December 4th, 2019, https://www.cbsnews.com/news/peloton-bike-ad-even-wall-street-hates-the-controversial-peloton-bike-ad-today-2019-12-05/.

Chatterjee, Sumeet & Anne Marie Roantree. "Mainland banks, pro-Beijing businesses caught in Hong Kong protest cross-hairs," *Reuters*, October 2nd, 2019, https://www.reuters.com/article/us-hongkong-protests-cleanup/mainland-banks-pro-beijing-businesses-caught-in-hong-kong-protest-cross-hairs -idUSKBN1WH055.

Chayefsky, Paddy. *Network,* DVD. Directed by Sidney Lumet, Metro-Goldwyn-Mayer, U.S.A., New York, 1976.

Clements, Jeffrey. *Corporations are not people: Why they have more rights that you do and what you can do about it.* San Francisco: Barrett-Koehler, 2012.

CNBC News. "'Bathroom bill' to cost North Carolina $3.76 billion," March 27th, 2017, https://www.cnbc.com/2017/03/27/bathroom-bill-to-cost-north-carolina-376-billion.html.

Coase, Ronald. "The Nature of the Firm." Economica 4, 16 (November 1937): pp. 386-405 https://doi.org/10.1111/j.1468-0335.1937.tb00002.x.

Coca-Cola HBC Magyarorszag. "Our impact in numbers." Coca-colahellenic. (Accessed December 12th 2019). https://hu.coca-colahellenic.com/en/local-impact/our-impact-in-numbers/.

Cohn, Scott. "Amazon reveals the truth on why it nixed NY and chose Virginia for HQ2," *CNBC,* July 10th, 2019, https://www.cnbc.com/2019/07/10/amazon-reveals-the-truth-on-why-it-nixed-ny-and-chose-virginia-for-hq2.html.

Cone. "2015 Cone Communications Millennial CSR Study." Conecomm.com. (Accessed February 17th 2019) https://www.conecomm.com/research-blog/2015-cone-communications-millennial-csr-study

Conger, Kate & Sheera Frenkel. "Dozens at Facebook unite to challenge its 'intolerant' liberal culture," *The New York Times,* August 28th, 2018, https://www.nytimes.com/2018/08/28/technology/inside-facebook-employees-political-bias.html.

Conor, Tim. "Time to scale up cooperation? Trade associations, NGOs, and the International Anti-Sweatshop Movement." *Development in Practice* 14, 1/2 (February 2004): pp. 61-70 doi: 10.1080/0961452032000170631.

Crane, Andrew, Dirk Matten & Jeremy Moon. *Corporations and Citizenship.* Cambridge: Cambridge University Press, 2008.

Crossley, Nick. "Global anti-corporate struggle: a preliminary analysis." *Br J Sociol* 53, 4 (December 2002): pp. 667–691 doi: 10.1080/0007131022000021542.

Crozier, Michael, Samuel P. Huntington & Joji Watanuki. *The Crisis of Democracy: Report on the Governability of Democracies to the Trilateral Commission.* New York: New York University Press, 1975.

Cui, Lin & Chungshik Moon. "What Attracts Foreign Direct Investment Into Autocratic States? Regime Time Horizon and Institutional Design." *The World Economy* 43, 10 (April 2020): pp. 2762-2784 https://doi.org/10.1111/twec.12956.

Danone. "Danone – One Planet, One Hope. Annual Report, 2017." Danone.com. (Accessed March 17th 2019) https://www.danone.com/integrated-annual-report-2019.html.

Danone. "Danone's dual commitment to business success and social progress." Prod.danone.emakina. (Accessed December 5th 2019) http://prod.danone.emakina.nbs-test.com/.

Daughtery, Owen. "Ryan Reynolds recruits actress from Peloton ad to troll fitness company's controversial commercial," *The Hill,* December 7th, 2019,

https://thehill.com/blogs/in-the-know/in-the-know/473510-ryan-reynolds
-recruits-actress-from-peloton-ad-to-troll-fitness.

Davies, Lizzy. "Pasta Firm Barilla Boycotted Over 'Classic Family' Remarks," *The Guardian*, September 26th, 2013, https://www.theguardian.com/world/2013/sep/26/pasta-firm-barilla-boycott-gay.

Davis, Jerry. "Why the NRA boycott has been so successful so quickly," *Business Insider*, March 3rd, 2018, https://www.businessinsider.com/why-nra-boycott-so-successful-so-quickly-2018-3.

Desanctis, Alexandra. "Judge Blocks Georgia's Pro-Life Heartbeat Bill," *National Review*, October 1st, 2019, https://www.nationalreview.com/corner/judge-blocks-georgia-heartbeat-bill/.

Dobuzinskis, Alex. "North Carolina 'bathroom bill' settlement approved," *Reuters*, July 23rd, 2019, https://www.reuters.com/article/us-north-carolina-lgbt/north-carolina-bathroom-bill-settlement-approved-idUSKCN1UI2IJ.

Douthat, Ross. "The Rise of Woke Capital," *New York Times*, February 28th, 2018, https://www.nytimes.com/2018/02/28/opinion/corporate-america-activism.html.

Draper, Kevin & Ken Belson. "Colin Kaepernick, Face of N.F.L. Protests, Is Face of New Nike Campaign," *New York Times*, September 3rd, 2018, https://www.nytimes.com/2018/09/03/sports/kaepernick-nike.html.

Edison Trends. "Nike Sales Grew 31% During Labor Day Weekend & Kaepernick Ad Campaign." Last updated September 7th 2018. https://trends.edison.tech/research/nike-labor-day-2018.html.

EIU. "Democracy Index 2020: In Sickness and in Health?" Pages.EIU.com (Accessed January 16th 2021) https://pages.eiu.com/rs/753-RIQ-438/images/democracy-index-2020.pdf?mkt_tok=eyJpIjoiT0dFeU9USTNOR1ppWlRneSIsInQiOiI0RmxteTd1K2xGN3hscFgzd1NWajY3RW9Bam84NmFteFVycDhxTkI0WjVXM0dsOFBXdzlQajVPYXFmemRUcEJyQjlsSHVibVwvc2dQeHBBQzlRT0RncFZZCU1Y5NXNwYWtRMnBSZklOVVhhG84Q2F0cjhzcnlamNUNUxzdUJuY0cifQ%3D%3D.

Ellis, Atiba R. "Citizens United and Tiered Personhood." *The John Marshall Law Review* 44, 3 (November, 2011): pp. 717-749.

Encyclopedia Britannica. "East India Company." Britannica.com. (Accessed February 22nd 2019) https://www.britannica.com/topic/East-India-Company.

Epstein, Adam. "'Regular guy' Donald Trump eats KFC with a knife and fork on his private jet," *Quartz*, August 2nd, 2016, https://qz.com/748241/regular-guy-donald-trump-eats-kfc-with-a-knife-and-fork-on-his-private-jet/.

Etter, Lauren, Vernon Silver & Sarah Frier. "How Facebook's Political Unit Enables the Dark Art of Digital Propaganda," *Bloomberg*, December 21st, 2017, https://www.bloomberg.com/news/features/2017-12-21/inside-the-facebook-team-helping-regimes-that-reach-out-and-crack-down.

Euronews. "Barilla, the company that is trying to tackle the climate crisis." Accessed December 15th 2019. https://www.euronews.com/2019/12/07/barilla-the-company-that-is-trying-to-tackle-the-climate-crisis.

Evans, Martin. "Man who attacked Nigel Farage with milkshake is ordered to pay cleaning bill after admitting assault charge," *Telegraph*, June 18th, 2019, https://www.telegraph.co.uk/news/2019/06/18/man-attacked-nigel-farage-milkshake-admits-assault-charge/.

Fang, Lee & Nick Surgey. "Chinese corporation Alibaba joins group ghostwriting American laws," *The Intercept*, March 20th, 2018, https://theintercept.com/2018/03/20/alibaba-chinese-corporation-alibaba-joins-group-ghostwriting-american-laws/.

Fineman, Joshua. "Peloton stock is pummeled on backlash from 'gift that gives' ad," *Fortune*, December 4th, 2019, https://fortune.com/2019/12/04/peloton-stock-falls-after-backlash-gift-that-gives-ad/.

Fischer, Sara. "Axios Harris Poll 100: Corporate trust soars during the pandemic," *Axios*, July 30th 2020, https://www.axios.com/coronavirus-clorox-amazon-disney-groceries-public-approval-bb24d50c-f77a-4e2e-ac2e-3760123b8755.html?utm_source=newsletter&utm_medium=email&utm_campaign=newsletter_axiosam&stream=top.

Folley, Aris. "Gucci advocates for women's rights to abortion on the runway," *The Hill*, May 29th, 2019, https://thehill.com/blogs/in-the-know/in-the-know/446067-gucci-advocates-for-womens-rights-to-abortion-on-the-runway.

Folley, Aris. "Nike's online sales surge after Kaepernick ads revealed," *The Hill*, September 7th, 2018, https://thehill.com/blogs/blog-briefing-room/news/405633-nikes-online-sales-surge-after-kaepernick-ads-revealed-report.

France24. "Hungary's Orban vows defence of 'Christian' Europe," February 10th, 2019, https://www.france24.com/en/20190210-hungarys-orban-vows-defence-christian-europe.

Fresh Air – NPR. "How American Corporations Had a 'Hidden' Civil Rights Movement," March 26th, 2018, https://www.npr.org/2018/03/26/596989664/how-american-corporations-had-a-hidden-civil-rights-movement.

Gallup. *"Party Affiliation."* News.Gallup.com. (Accessed October 12th 2019). https://news.gallup.com/poll/15370/party-affiliation.aspx

Geltzer, Josh & Lydia Wheeler. "Judge Rules Trump Cannot Block Users on Twitter," *The Hill*, May 23rd, 2018, https://thehill.com/policy/technology/452160-appeals-court-rules-trump-cant-block-people-on-twitter.

Gibson, Kate. "Colin Kaepernick is Nike's $6 billion man," *CBS News*, September 21st, 2018, https://www.cbsnews.com/news/colin-kaepernick-nike-6-billion-man/.

Goldberg, Jonah. *Liberal Fascism: The Secret History of the American Left, From Mussolini to the Politics of Change*. London: Random House, 2009.

Grim, Ryan & Glenn Greenwald. "U.S. Senate's first bill, in the midst of shutdown, is a bipartisan defense of the Israeli government from boycotts," *The Intercept*, January 5th, 2019, https://theintercept.com/2019/01/05/u-s-senates-first-bill-in-midst-of-shutdown-is-a-bipartisan-defense-of-the-israeli-government-from-boycotts/.

Grim, Ryan. "Elizabeth Warren unveils radical anti-corruption platform," *The Intercept*, August 21st, 2018, https://theintercept.com/2018/08/21/elizabeth-warren-unveils-radical-anti-corruption-platform/.

Grimsley, Kristin Downey. "McDonald's restaurants going smoke-free," *The Washington Post*, February 24th, 1994, https://www.washingtonpost.com/

archive/politics/1994/02/24/mcdonalds-restaurants-going-smoke-free/a30
8b6e6-53b4-4451-b364-5c10739ab723/.

Gross, Liza. "Smoke Screen: Big Vape is copying Big Tobacco's playbook," *The Verge*, November 16th, 2017, https://www.theverge.com/2017/11/16/16658358/vape-lobby-vaping-health-risks-nicotine-big-tobacco-marketing.

Gross, Terry. "How Drug Companies Helped Shape a Shifting, Biological view of Mental Illness," *NPR*, May 2nd, 2019, https://www.npr.org/sections/health-shots/2019/05/02/718744068/how-drug-companies-helped-shape-a-shifting-biological-view-of-mental-illness.

Gstalter, Morgan. "Michigan 18-year-old sues Dick's over new gun age rule," *The Hill*, March 9th, 2018, https://thehill.com/blogs/blog-briefing-room/news/377597-michigan-18-year-old-sues-dicks-over-new-gun-age-rule.

Gura, David. "Mad about corporate donations, customers boycott Target, Best Buy," *NPR*, August 4th, 2010, https://www.npr.org/sections/thetwo-way/2010/08/04/128974389/mad-about-corporate-political-donations-customers-boycott-target-best-buy.

Haas, Benjamin. "Marriott apologises to China over Tibet and Taiwan error," *The Guardian*, January 12th, 2018, https://www.theguardian.com/world/2018/jan/12/marriott-apologises-to-china-over-tibet-and-taiwan-error.

Hafner, Josh. "Louisiana mayor rescinds Nike ban after blowback from community and advice from attorney," *USA Today*, September 14th, 2018, https://eu.usatoday.com/story/money/nation-now/2018/09/13/nike-ban-mayor-dropped-louisiana-advice-city-attorney/1292137002/.

Hart, Oliver & Luigi Zingales. "Companies should maximize shareholder welfare not market value." *Journal of Law, Finance and Accounting* 2, 2 (2017): pp. 247-274.

Hellman, Deborah. "Money Talks but it isn't Speech." *Minnesota Law Review* 102, 6 (2011): pp. 953-1002.

Hern, Alex. "Tim Cook defends Apple's removal of Hong Kong mapping app," *The Guardian*, October 10th, 2019, https://www.theguardian.com/technology/2019/oct/10/tim-cook-apple-hong-kong-mapping-app-removal.

Hertz, Noreena. "Better to shop than to vote?" *Business Ethics: A European Review* 10, 3 (2001): pp. 190-193 https://doi.org/10.1111/1467-8608.00232

Hobbes, Thomas. *Leviathan*, (1651) https://www.gutenberg.org/files/3207/3207-h/3207-h.htm#link2H_4_0048.

Horowitz, Julia. "Trump: Nike's Clin Kaepernick campaign sends 'terrible message'," *CNN*, September 4th, 2018, https://money.cnn.com/2018/09/04/news/companies/trump-nike-kaepernick/index.html.

Hsu, Tiffany. "Gap, Wary of Crossing China, Apologizes for T-Shirt's Map," *The New York Times*, May 15th, 2018, https://www.nytimes.com/2018/05/15/business/gap-china-apology.html.

Hunt, Joshua. "Colin Kaepernick, Nike, and the myth of good and bad companies," *The Atlantic*, September 5th, 2018, https://www.theatlantic.com/business/archive/2018/09/nike-kaepernick/569371/.

Institute of Medicine (US) Committee on Secondhand Smoke Exposure and Acute Coronary Events. "Secondhand Smoke Exposure and Cardiovascular Effects: Making Sense of the Evidence." National Academies Press, 2010.

Ivie, Devon. "The Peloton Husband Is Worried That His Acting Career Is Dead," *Vulture*, December 8th, 2019, https://www.vulture.com/2019/12/peloton-ad-husband-is-worried-that-his-acting-career-is-dead.html.

Jacobs, Frank. "Climate change: 100 CEOs killing the planet," *Big Think*, May 6th, 2019, https://bigthink.com/strange-maps/climate-change.

Jeurissen, Ronald. "Institutional conditions of corporate citizenship." *Journal of Business Ethics* 53, (August 2004): pp. 87-96.

Kaszas, Fanni. "Coca-Cola Fined for Ads with Same-Sex Couples 'Undermining Adolescents' Moral Development'," *Hungary Today*, October 15th, 2019, https://hungarytoday.hu/coca-cola-fined-for-ads-with-same-sex-couples-undermining-adolescents-moral-development/.

Keller, Megan. "Trump Jr. says he'd back a new conservative version of Facebook," *The Hill*, May 30th, 2018, https://thehill.com/policy/technology/404326-trump-jr-says-hed-back-a-new-conservative-version-of-facebook.

Keller, Megan. "Twitter CEO Jack Dorsey: Conservative employees don't feel safe to express their opinions," *The Hill*, September 16th, 2018, https://thehill.com/policy/technology/406927-twitter-ceo-jack-dorsey-conservative-employees-dont-feel-safe-to-express.

Kelley, Alexandra. "Nike Inc. announces $40 million donation to black community organizations," *The Hill*, June 5th, 2020, https://thehill.com/changing-america/respect/equality/501369-nike-inc-announces-40-million-donation-to-black-community?fbclid=IwAR27LrLkX0HoXwAtPXTR16xQUhTVM5qwD0NcQxFnDKm5gKu3K2hfCFieYLo.

Kelly, Makena. "Immigration nonprofit refuses $250,000 Salesforce donation over its contract with US government," *The Verge*, July 19th, 2018, https://www.theverge.com/2018/7/19/17590240/immigration-non-profit-raices-refuses-salesforce-donation.

Kelly, Mary Louise. "Mattel introduces 17 'Shero' Barbies to celebrate international women's day," *NPR*, March 8th, 2018, https://www.npr.org/2018/03/08/592046301/mattel-introduces-shero-barbies-for-international-womens-day.

Kesslen, Ben. "Gillette is woke now? When brands try to keep up with the times," *Euronews*, January 15th, 2019, https://www.euronews.com/2019/01/15/gillette-woke-now-when-brands-try-keep-times-n958996.

Khomami, Nadia & Jessica Gleza. "'Try Again': McDonald's women's day stunt criticized as hollow gesture," *The Guardian*, March 8th, 2018, https://www.theguardian.com/business/2018/mar/08/mcdonalds-sign-international-womens-day.

Khumalo, Boniswa. "Heineken gets backlash for racist lighter is better ad," *ENCA*, March 31st, 2018, https://www.enca.com/life/watch-heineken-gets-backlash-for-racist-lighter-is-better-ad.

LaChance, Naomi. "More Nazis are Getting Identified and Fired after Charlottesville," *Huffington Post*, August 16th, 2017, https://www.huffpost.com/entry/more-nazis-are-getting-identified-and-fired-after-charlottesville_b_599477dbe4b0eef7ad2c0318.

Ladd, Jonathan M, Joshua A. Tucker & Sean Kates. "2018 American Institutional Confidence: The Health of American Democracy in an era of hyper-polarization." *Baker Center for Leadership & Governance.* (Accessed December 3rd 2019). http://aicpoll.com/.

Le Textier, Thibault. "Interview of author and professor Alain Supiot." *Espirit*, April 13th, 2018, https://www.eurozine.com/economic-democracy-interview -alain-supiot/.

Li, Pei & Adam Jourdan. "Mercedes-Benz apologizes to Chinese for quoting Dalai Lama," *Business Insider*, February 6th, 2018, https://www.reuters.com/ article/us-mercedes-benz-china-gaffe/mercedes-benz-apologizes-to-chine se-for-quoting-dalai-lama-idUSKBN1FQ1FJ.

Lochhead, Colton. "Bill would allow tech companies to create local governments." *Las Vegas Review-Journal*, February 3rd, 2021, https://www. reviewjournal.com/news/politics-and-government/2021-legislature/bill- would-allow-tech-companies-to-create-local-governments-2272887/.

Lorenz, Taylor. "The End Finally Comes for Alex Jones," *The Atlantic*, September 7th, 2018, https://www.theatlantic.com/technology/archive/2018/09/the- end-finally-comes-for-alex-jones/569578/.

Ludwig, Kirk. "Corporate Speech in Citizens United vs. Federal Election Commission," *Spazio Filosofico*, 2016, https://www.spaziofilosofico.it/en/ numero-16/6059/corporate-speech-in-citizens-united-vs-federal-election- commission/.

March, James. "The Business Firm as a Political Coalition." *The Journal of Politics* 24, 4 (November 1962): pp. 662-678 https://doi.org/10.2307/2128040

Marist Poll. "NPR/PBS NewsHour/Marist Poll Results January 2018." MaristPoll.Marist.edu. (Accessed February 10th 2019). http://maristpoll. marist.edu/nprpbs-newshourmarist-poll-results-january-2018/#sthash.r6H LsX9E.dpbs.

Marshall, T.H. *Citizenship and Social Class and Other Essays.* New York: Cambridge University Press, 1950.

Martis, Jharonne. "Nike ad spurs 61% rise in sold out items," *Refinitiv*, September 19th, 2018, https://lipperalpha.refinitiv.com/2018/09/nike-ad- spurs-61-rise-in-sold-out-items/.

Mazza, Ed. "Haters mocked for wrecking their stuff to protest Kaepernick deal," *Huffington Post*, September 9th, 2018, https://www.huffpost.com/entry/nike -colin-kaepernick-protest_n_5.

McAllister, Emily J., Nikhil V. Dhurandhar, Scott W. Keith, Louis J. Aronne, Jamie Barger, Monica Baskin, Ruth M. Benca, Joseph Biggio, Mary M. Boggiano, Joe C. Eisenmann, Mai Elobeid, Kevin R. Fontaine, Peter Gluckman, Erin C. Hanlon, Peter Katzmarzyk, Angelo Pietrobelli, David T. Redden, Douglas M. Ruden, Chenxi Wang, Robert A. Waterland, Suzanne M. Wright, David B. Allison. "Ten putative contributors to the obesity epidemic." *Crit. Rev. Food Sci. Nutr* 49, 10 (November 2009): pp. 868-931 https://doi.org/10.1080/ 10408390903372599.

McArdle, Megan. "Why you should care about the Supreme Court's Janus decision," *The Washington Post*, June 27th, 2018, https://www.washington post.com/opinions/the-supreme-court-may-have-killed-collective-bargaini ng/2018/06/27/9b19bbc6-7a3c-11e8-aeee-4d04c8ac6158_story.html.

McDonald, Samantha. "Adidas pulls 'black history month' sneakers amid 'all-white' color criticism," *FootWearNews*, February 1st, 2019, https://footwear news.com/2019/focus/athletic-outdoor/adidas-back-history-month-sneak ers-cbc-pulled-1202737846/.

Medium. "A walk through Danone's history," November 21st, 2016, https:// medium .com/@Danone/a-walk-through-the-danones-history-a031acdb7335.

Micklethwait, John & Adrian Wooldridge. *The Company: A Short History of A Revolutionary Idea*. New York & Toronto: Random House Canada, 2003.

Mill, John Stuart. *Considerations on Representative Government*. Cambridge: Cambridge University Press, 2010.

Millhiser, Ian. "Justice Kennedy deserves this nasty, unflinching sendoff," *Think Progress*, June 27th, 2018, https://thinkprogress.org/kennedy-was-a-bad-justice-76e464024d78/.

Mises, Ludwig von. *Interventionism: An Economic Analysis*. Liberty Fund, 1998 (1940).

Montopoli, Brian. "Target boycott movement grows following donation to support 'antigay' candidate," *CBS News*, July 28th, 2010, https://www. cbsnews.com/news/target-boycott-movement-grows-following-donation-to-support-antigay-candidate/.

Moon, Jeremy, Andrew Crane & Dirk Matten. "Can corporations be citizens? Corporate citizenship as a metaphor for business participation in society." *Business Ethics Quarterly* 15, 3 (July 2005): pp. 429-453 https://doi.org/ 10.5840/beq200515329.

Moser, Richard. "How Corporate Power Killed Democracy," *CounterPunch*, December 6th, 2017, https://www.counterpunch.org/2017/12/06/how-corporate-power-killed-democracy/.

Nasdaq. "Adidas (ADDYY)." Nasdaq.com. (Accessed November 1st 2019). https://www.nasdaq.com/market-activity/stocks/addyy/historical.

Nasdaq. "Nike Inc. (NKE) NYSE." Nasdaq.com. (Accessed November 1st 2019). https://www.nasdaq.com/market-activity/stocks/nke/historical.

Nasdaq. "Tiffany & Co. (TIF) NYSE." Nasdaq.com. (Accessed November 1st 2019). https://www.nasdaq.com/market-activity/stocks/tif.

Nazario, Marina & Dylan Roach. "Nike's incredible road to becoming the world's dominant sneaker retailer," *Business Insider*, October 4th, 2015, https://www.businessinsider.com.au/nike-history-timeline-2015-10.

Nedelmann, Michael. "Ambien maker Sanofi: 'Racism is not a known side effect'," *CNN*, May 30th, 2018, https://edition.cnn.com/2018/05/30/health/ ambien-roseanne-barr-racist-tweets-bn/index.html.

Neron, Pierre-Yves. "Business and the Polis: What Does it Mean to See Corporations as Political Actors?" *Journal of Business Ethnics* 94, 3 (November 2009): pp. 333-352.

Neron, Pierre-Yves. "Rethinking the Ethics of Corporate Political Activities in Post-Citizens United Era: Political Equality, Corporate Citizenship and Market Failures." *Journal of Business Ethics* 136 (October 2015): pp. 715-728.

Nestle. "Why was a Nestle boycott launched?" Netle.com. (Accessed December 13th 2018) https://www.nestle.com/ask-nestle/our-company/answers/nestle-boycott.

Nicholson, Walter & Christopher Snyder. *Microeconomic Theory: Basic Principles and Extensions.* Mason: Thomson South-Western, 2008.

Novak, Matt. "Apple Sells Out Pro-Democracy Protesters in Hong Kong to Appease Chinese Government," *Gizmondo,* October 10th, 2019, https://gizmodo.com/apple-sells-out-pro-democracy-protesters-in-hong-kong-t-1838932096.

Oatley, Thomas. *International Political Economy.* New York & London: Routledge, 2019.

Padfield, Stefan. "Rehabilitating Concession Theory." *Oklahoma Law Review* 66, 2 (2013): pp. 327-361.

Patagonia. "Environmental & Social Responsibility." Patagonia.com (Accessed December 3rd 2019) https://www.patagonia.com/environmentalism.html.

Peretti, Jacques. "Fat profits: how the good industry cashed in on obesity," *The Guardian,* August 7th, 2013, https://www.theguardian.com/lifeandstyle/2013/aug/07/fat-profits-food-industry-obesity.

Phillips, Amber. "Georgia Republicans are crossing an ethically murky line by threatening Delta over its NRA boycott," *The Washington Post,* February 27th, 2018, https://www.washingtonpost.com/news/the-fix/wp/2018/02/27/georgia-republicans-are-crossing-an-ethically-murky-line-by-threatening-delta-over-its-nra-boycott/.

Phillips, Michael. "Reappraising the Real Entity Theory of the Corporation." *Florida State University Law Review* 21, 4 (Spring 1994): pp. 1061-1123.

Pitkin, Hanna Fenichel. *The Concept of Representation.* Berkeley: University of California Press, 1967.

Pitofsky, Marina. "Chick-fil-A closing first UK restaurant after protests," *The Hill,* October 19th 2019, https://thehill.com/blogs/blog-briefing-room/news/466604-Chick-fil-A-closing-first-uk-restaurant-after-protests.

Plattner, Marc. "Populism, pluralism and liberal democracy." *Journal of Democracy* 21, 1 (January 2010): pp. 81-92 https://doi.org/10.1353/jod.0.0154

Politico. "Did US Justice Anthony Kennedy Just Destroy His Own Legacy?" July 28th, 2018, https://www.politico.eu/article/did-us-supreme-court-justice-anthony-kennedy-just-destroy-his-own-legacy/.

Powell, Lewis F. Jr. "Confidential Memorandum   Attack on American Free Enterprise System." Washington and Lee University Scholarly Commons. (Accessed June 3rd 2018). https://scholarlycommons.law.wlu.edu/powell memo/.

Procter & Gamble (PG) NYSE common stock historical data available at www.nasdaq.com, accessed on the 20th of November 2019.

Rand, Ayn. *Capitalism, The Unknown Ideal.* New York: Penguin, 1946.

Reinicke, Carmen. "Peloton saw $942 million in market value wiped out in a single day amid backlash to its controversial holiday ad," *BusinessInsider,* December 4th, 2019, https://markets.businessinsider.com/news/stocks/pelotons-stock-price-plummet-wiped-942-million-market-value-holiday-ad-2019-12-1028737428.

Riddell, John. *To the masses: Proceedings of the Third Congress of the Communist International, 1921.* Leiden & Boston: Brill, 2014.

Rinner, William. "Maximizing Participation Through Campaign Finance Regulation: A Cap and Trade Mechanism for Political Money." *The Yale Law Journal* 119, 5 (March 2010): pp. 848-1121.

Roark, Cortney. "Nickelodeon went off the air for 17 minutes at the time of the national walkout," *USA Today Network*, March 14th, 2018, https://eu. usatoday.com/story/life/nation-now/2018/03/14/nickelodeon-went-off-air -17-minutes-national-walkout/424430002/.

Roberts, Joe. "Burger King accused of 'inciting violence' against Farage by selling milkshakes," *MetroNews*, May 19th, 2019, https://metro.co.uk/2019/ 05/19/burger-king-accused-inciting-violence-farage-selling-milkshakes-95 98586/.

Ross, Bertrall II. "Addressing Inequality in the Age of Citizens United." *New York University Law Review* 93, 5 (2018): pp. 1132-1135.

Sarner, Moya. "Inequality at 30,000 feet: is aviation the least progressive industry?" *The Guardian*, March 6th, 2018, https://www.theguardian.com/ world/shortcuts/2018/mar/06/inequality-30000-feet-qantas-aviation-least-progressive-industry.

Savov, Vlad & Mark Gurman. "Apple Pulls App That Tracks Police Activity in Hong Kong," *Bloomberg*, October 10th, 2019, https://www.bloomberg.com/ news/articles/2019-10-10/apple-reverses-course-again-bans-controversial-hong-kong-app.

Shear, Michael D. & Cecilia Kang. "Amazon has lots of company as Trump slams 'stupid' businesses," *New York Times*, April 3rd 2018, https://www.nytimes. com/2018/04/03/us/politics/trump-amazon.html.

Shelbourne, Mallory. "Trump: 'Dirty' restaurant that refused to serve Sanders 'needs a paint job'," *The Hill*, June 25th, 2018, https://thehill.com/ homenews/administration/393900-trump-dirty-restaurant-that-refused-sanders-needs-a-paint-job.

Somashekhar, Sandhya. "Human Rights campaign says Barilla has turned around its policies on LGBT," *The Washington Post*, November 19th, 2014, https://www.washingtonpost.com/politics/human-rights-campaign-says-barilla-has-turned-around-its-policies-on-lgbt/2014/11/18/9866efde-6e92-11e4-8808-afaa1e3a33ef_story.html.

Sonnad, Nikhil. "Versace is the latest major brand to express its 'deepest apologies' to China," *Quartz*, August 11th, 2019, https://qz.com/1685587/ versace-the-latest-brand-to-express-deepest-apologies-to-china/.

Sowell, Thomas. *Basic Economics: A Citizen's Guide to the Economy*. New York: Perseus Books, 2000.

Stelter, Brian & Shannon Liao. "Disney, Netflix and WarnerMedia say new abortion law may push their movies out of Georgia," *CNN Business*, May 30th, 2019, https://edition.cnn.com/2019/05/30/business/disney-bob-iger-abor tion-georgia/index.html.

Suen, Zoe. "Vans Competition Pulls Sneaker Brand Into Hong Kong Political Row," *Business of Fashion*, October 4th, 2019, https://www.businessoffashion .com/articles/news-analysis/vans-competition-pulls-sneaker-brand-into-hong-kong-political-row.

Sun, Feng. "The Dual Political Effects of Foreign Direct Investment in Developing Countries." *The Journal of Developing Areas* 48, 1 (Winter 2014): pp. 107-125 https://doi.org/10.1353/jda.2014.0020.

Sydell, Laura. "Tech Workers Demand CEOs Stop Doing Business with ICE, Other U.S. Agencies," *NPR*, July 14th, 2018, https://www.npr.org/2018/07/14/628765208/tech-workers-demand-ceos-stop-doing-business-with-ice-other-u-s-agencies.

Taylor, Kate. "Chick-fil-A likely loses out on more than $1 billion in sales every year by closing on Sundays — and it's a brilliant business strategy," *Business Insider*, July 29th, 2019, https://www.businessinsider.com/Chick-fil-A-closes-on-sunday-why-2019-7.

The Daily Show with Trevor Noah, "Nike's Kaepernick Ad – Between the Scenes," YouTube video, 2:05, September 5th 2018, https://www.youtube.com/watch?v=nma4GJ2rfwU&ab_channel=TheDailyShowwithTrevorNoah.

The Economist. "American companies snub the National Rifle Association," March 1st, 2018, https://www.economist.com/business/2018/03/01/american-companies-snub-the-national-rifle-association.

The Economist. "Danone rethinks the idea of the firm," August 9th, 2018, https://www.economist.com/business/2018/08/09/danone-rethinks-the-idea-of-the-firm.

The Economist. "What if the unwashed masses got to vote on companies' strategies?" November 30th, 2017, https://www.economist.com/business/2017/11/30/what-if-the-unwashed-masses-got-to-vote-on-companies-strategies.

The Guardian. "Pro-LGBT Coca-Cola adverts spark boycott calls in Hungary," August 5th, 2019, https://www.theguardian.com/world/2019/aug/05/pro-lgbt-coca-cola-ads-spark-boycott-calls-in-hungary.

TheChickenWire. "Chick-fil-A Foundation announces 2020 priorities to address education, homelessness and education," November 18th, 2019, https://thechickenwire.Chick-fil-A.com/news/Chick-fil-A-foundation-announces-2020-priorities.

Thorbecke, Catherine. "Chick-fil-A will no longer fund organizations with anti-LGBTQ ties," *ABC News*, November 19th, 2019, https://abcnews.go.com/Business/chick-fil-longer-fund-anti-lgbtq-organizations/story?id=67111125.

Tiffany. "What Is Tiffany Doing About The Problem Of Conflict Diamonds?" Tiffany.com. (Accessed January 9th 2019) https://www.tiffany.com/faq/a-tiffany-diamond-faq/what-is-tiffany-doing-about-the-problem-of-conflict-diamond/.

Timberg, Craig, Tony Romm, Devlin Barrett & Brian Fung. "Justice Department warns tech companies as Facebook and Twitter defend themselves in Congress," *Washington Post*, September 6th, 2018, https://www.washingtonpost.com/technology/2018/09/05/justice-department-consider-allegations-censorship-facebook-twitter/.

Toh, Michelle & Laura He. "Nike pulls products in China after designer sparks social media outrage," *CNN*, June 27th, 2019, https://edition.cnn.com/2019/06/27/business/nike-china-japan-hong-kong/index.html.

Tribe, Laurence. "Dividing 'Citizens United': The Case v. The Controversy." *Constitutional Commentary* 30, 2 (Summer 2015): pp. 463-494.

Tuttle, Brad. "All the advertisers dropping Laura Ingraham after she mocked Parkland survivor David Hogg," *Money.com*, March 30th, 2018, https://money.com/laura-ingraham-david-hogg-advertising-boycott/.

Ungureanu, Mihai, Alexandru Volacu & Andra Roescu. *Alegere rationala si comportament* electoral. Bucharest: Tritonic-IPP, 2015.

Victor, Daniel. "Pepsi Pulls Ad Accused of Trivializing Black Lives Matter," *The New York Times*, April 5th, 2017, https://www.nytimes.com/2017/04/05/business/kendall-jenner-pepsi-ad.html.

Vogel, David. "The Power of Business in America: A Re-appraisal." *British Journal of Political Science* 13, 1 (January 1983): pp. 19-43 https://doi.org/10.1017/S0007123400003124.

Waltzer, Michael. *Obligations. Essays on Disobedience, War and Citizenship.* Cambridge & London: Harvard University Press, 1982.

Wang, Amy. "Wal-Mart pulls Cosmopolitan from checkout aisles after pressure from anti-porn group," *The Washington Post*, March 28th, 2018, https://www.washingtonpost.com/news/business/wp/2018/03/28/walmart-pulls-cosmopolitan-from-checkout-aisles-after-pressure-from-anti-porn-group/.

Washington Post. "Final Trump-Clinton Debate Transcript for the 2016 presidential elections," October 20th, 2016, https://www.washingtonpost.com/news/the-fix/wp/2016/10/19/the-final-trump-clinton-debate-transcript-annotated/.

Wattles, Jackie & Rene Marsh. "Airlines ask the government not to fly separated children on their planes," *CNN Money*, June 20th, 2018, https://money.cnn.com/2018/06/20/news/companies/american-airlines-children-detention-border-trump/index.html.

Weber, Max. *The Protestant Ethic and the Spirit of Capitalism.* London: Routledge, 2001.

West, Samantha. "H&M faced backlash over its 'monkey' sweatshirt ad. It isn't the company's only controversy," *The Washington Post*, January 19th, 2018, https://www.washingtonpost.com/news/arts-and-entertainment/wp/2018/01/19/hm-faced-backlash-over-its-monkey-sweatshirt-ad-it-isnt-the-companys-only-controversy/.

Williams, Charles Richard & Rutherford Birchard Hayes. *Diary and Letters of Rutherford Birchard Hayes: Nineteenth President of the United States.* Ulan Press, 2012 (1923).

Winkler, Adam. "'Corporations Are People' is built on an incredible 19th-century lie," *The Atlantic*, March 5th, 2018, https://www.theatlantic.com/business/archive/2018/03/corporations-people-adam-winkler/554852/.

Winkler, Adam. *We the Corporations: How American Businesses Won Their Civil Rights.* London & New York: W.W. Norton & Company, 2018.

World Bank. "Country Data – China." WorldBank.org. (Accessed December 30th 2019). https://data.worldbank.org/country/china.

World Bank. "Development Indicators" WorldBank.org. (Accessed December 8th 2019). http://datatopics.worldbank.org/world-development-indicators/.

Yeung, Jessie. "Vans faces Hong Kong boycott over sneaker design controversy," *CNN*, October 7th, 2019, https://edition.cnn.com/style/article/vans-hong-kong-intl-hnk-scli/index.html.

Yu, Verna. "'Protecting rioters': China warns Apple over app that tracks Hong Kong police," *The Guardian*, October 9th, 2019, https://www.theguardian.com/world/2019/oct/09/protecting-rioters-china-warns-apple-over-app-that-tracks-hong-kong-police.

Zenz, Adrian. "Xinjiang's New Slavery," *Foreign Policy*, December 11th, 2019, https://foreignpolicy.com/2019/12/11/cotton-china-uighur-labor-xinjiang-new-slavery/.

Legal Documents

- *Austin* v. *Michigan Chamber of Commerce*, 494 U. S. 652 (1990)

- *Buckley v. Valeo*, 424 U.S. 1 (1976)

- *Burwell* v. *Hobby Lobby Stores, Inc.*, 573 U.S. (2014)

- *Citizens United* v. *FEC*, 558 U.S. 310 (2010)

- Federal Election Campaign Act Amendments of 1974

- *First Nat. Bank of Boston* v. *Bellotti*, 435 U. S. 765, 778 (1978)

- *Grosjean* v. *American Press Co.*, 297 U. S. 233, 244 (1936)

- *McConnell* v. *Federal Election Commission*, 540 U. S. 93, 203–209 (2003)

- *Parker* v. *Levy*, 417 U. S. 733, 759 (1974)

- *United States* v. *Playboy Entertainment Group, Inc.*, 529 U. S. 803, 813 (2000)

Index

A

Abood v. Detroit Board of Education, 8
Adam Winkler
  Winkler, 13, 18, 21, 22, 23, 24, 32, 131
Adidas, 66, 89, 90, 127
Adrian Wooldridge, 1, 2, 3
  Wooldridge, 3, 127
Africa, 28, 29, 57, 79
agency shop, 8
Airbnb, 77, 78, 119
Alain Supiot, 31, 126
  Supiot, 31
Alex Jones, 92, 93, 95, 126
  Jones, 92, 93
Alibaba, 47, 123
amalgamation theory, 16
Amazon, 33, 41, 69, 71, 97, 119, 121, 129
Ambien, 92, 127
American Airlines, 54
Amgen, 40
Anthony Downs, 50
Anthony Kennedy, 5, 7, 128
  Kennedy, 5, 6, 7, 8, 12, 13, 127
Apple, vi, 69, 95, 103, 108, 109, 124, 128, 129, 132
Aristotle, 37, 50
Armani, 84
artificial persons, 18, 21, 30, 32, 75, 99, 116
AT&T, vii, 1, 85, 97
Atlanta, 63, 71, 85
Austin, 5, 10, 11, 12, 132
Austin v. Michigan Chamber of Commerce
  Austin, 5, 11, 132
Australia, 53
Aviation Gin, 88
Ayn Rand, 46

B

Bank of China, 108
Bank of the United States v. *Deveaux*, 13
Barbie, 54
Barilla, 30, 44, 51, 62, 63, 64, 122, 129
bathroom bill, 66, 122
Benito Mussolini, 114, 115, 123
Best Buy, 65, 66, 67, 124
Biotechnology Innovations Organization, 40
Black Lives Matter, 59, 131
Boston Tea Party, 2
Botswana, 78
BP, 27
Breitbart, 93
Brexit, 71, 72
Brown v. *Board of Education*, 24
Buckley v. Valeo
  Buckley, 6, 8, 10, 18, 132
Burger King, 72, 117, 129
buyers' market, ix
BuzzFeed, 93

C

California, 3, 16, 21, 35, 42, 56, 128
capitalism, ix, 33, 35, 43, 45, 46,
    114
Casey Cagle, 70, 71, 83
Charlottesville, 44, 94, 125
Chevron Corporation, 49
Chick-fil-A, 63, 64, 120, 130
Chief Justice Roberts, 12
China, 1, 103, 104, 105, 106, 107,
    108, 109, 110, 113, 119, 124, 129,
    130, 131, 132
Citizens United, v, vi, viii, ix, 5, 6, 7,
    8, 10, 11, 12, 13, 15, 16, 17, 18,
    21, 23, 27, 30, 33, 38, 39, 40, 60,
    65, 74, 75, 116, 122, 126, 127,
    130, 132
    Citizens United v. FEC, 7, 12
CNN, 55, 80, 84, 85, 92, 97, 110,
    124, 127, 129, 130, 131, 132
Coca-Cola, 30, 37, 67, 121, 125, 130
Code of Bills and Statues, 6
Colin Kaepernick, 10, 65, 79, 80,
    81, 83, 122, 123, 124
    Kaepernick, 29, 79, 80, 81, 82,
        83, 89, 100, 122, 123, 124, 126,
        130
Colonel Sanders, 56, 120
concession theory, 15, 16, 22, 28
Corporate citizenship, 25, 27, 127
corporate social responsibility, x,
    26
corporate-led democracy, v, 105,
    113
Cosmopolitan, 60, 61, 131
CoStar, 66
*County of Santa Clara v. Southern
    Pacific Rail*, 16
Crystal City, 71

D

daily plebiscite, ix, x, 42, 52
Dalai Lama, 105, 126
Danone, 85, 86, 121, 127, 130
David Hogg, 73, 74, 131
Deborah Hellman
    Hellman, 8, 9, 124
Delta, 54, 70, 71, 77, 83, 107, 128
Democratic Party, 38, 41, 49, 50,
    51, 67, 74, 82, 84, 118
Democrats, 48, 49, 50, 75, 100
deregulation, 24, 100
Deutsche Bank, 66
Diana J. Humetewa, 75
Disney, 84, 85, 119, 129
Dolce & Gabbana, 84
Donald Trump, vi, 43, 73, 91, 93,
    94, 97, 98, 100, 101, 122
    Trump, 17, 44, 54, 76, 80, 91, 97,
        98, 99, 100, 119, 123, 124, 125,
        129, 131

E

East India Trading Company, 2, 3,
    28
Eastern Europe, 28
Edinburgh, 72
Edmund Burke, 43
Elizabeth Heyrick, 2, 58, 64
environmentalism, 55
Europe, 31, 58, 66, 67, 86, 98, 103,
    107, 119, 123
Expedia, 73
ExxonMobil, 27
    Exxon, vii, 27

F

Facebook, vi, 41, 44, 45, 91, 92, 93, 94, 95, 98, 119, 121, 122, 125, 130
FB'ers for Political Diversity, 91
Federal Election Committee, v, viii, 10, 11, 12
FedEx, 69
Fellowship of Christian Athletes, 64
Fila, 116
First Amendment, 5, 6, 7, 9, 10, 11, 12, 13, 17, 24, 38, 75, 98
First National Bank of Boston v. Belloti, 7
First National Bank of Omaha, 68
Founding Fathers, 23, 79, 101
Fourteenth Amendment, 16, 21, 22
Frontier Airlines, 54

G

Gap, 106, 124
gender equality, 56, 84, 118
Georgia, 33, 70, 71, 83, 84, 85, 119, 122, 128, 129
Gillette, 30, 58, 59, 60, 61, 86, 89, 119, 125
Google, 33, 41, 94, 118
Great Britain, 2, 43
Grosjean v. American Press, 7, 132
Guantanamo Bay, 8
Gucci, 83, 84, 123

H

H&M, 29, 57, 58, 131
habeas corpus, 8
Hanna Pitkin, 42, 43, 128

Harvard University, 39, 62, 131
Harvey Weinstein, 58
Hegel, 39
HEIC, 2, 3, *See* East India Trading Company
Heineken, 30, 57, 58, 125
Hillary Clinton, 5, 6, 38
Hobby Lobby, 13, 23, 132
Hong Kong, 105, 106, 107, 108, 109, 110, 119, 120, 124, 128, 129, 132
Howard Beale, vii
    Beale, vii
Human Rights Watch, 78
Hungary, 66, 67, 98, 123, 125, 130

I

ICE, 33, 35, 130
India, 1, 3, 28, 70, 122
Indian Mutiny, 3
Instagram, 105, 109
Iran, 61, 62
Ivanka Trump, 97, 119

J

J.C. Bancroft Davis, 22
Jack Dorsey, 95, 120, 125
Janus v. AFCME, 9
Jeff Bezos, 71, 97
Jeffrey D. Clements
    Clements, 28, 29, 30, 31, 121
Jeremy Corbyn, 43
John Adams, 43
John Micklethwait, 1, 2, 3
    Micklethwait, 3, 127
Johnny Walker, 56
Johnson & Johnson, 73
Justice Anthony Scalia, 11

Justice Lewis Powell, 45
Justice Stevens, 10
   Stevens, 10, 11

K

Karl Marx, 39
KFC, 56, 100, 101, 120, 122
Koch brothers, 51

L

Laura Ingraham, 73, 74, 120, 131
   Ingraham, 73, 74, 75, 76
Laurence H. Tribe
   Tribe, 11, 12, 130
LGBTQ, 33, 63, 64, 78, 130
liberal democracy, 8, 51, 79, 105,
   115, 116, 128
Limehouse & Sons, 44, 94
Lockton and Chubb, 68
Louis Vuitton, 84
Ludwig von Mises, ix
   Mises, ix, x, 127
Lyft, 75, 76, 119, 120

M

Macau, 105, 106
Malaysia, 56, 120
Margaret Thatcher, 24, 33
Marjory Stoneman Douglas, 68
Marriot, 103
Massachusets Company, 2
Masterpiece Cakeshop, 8
Mattel, 54, 55, 125
Mauritius, 79
McConnell, 5, 10, 132
McDonald's, 29, 55, 56, 72, 103,
   107, 117, 123, 125

Mercedes-Benz, 103, 105, 126
Mesopotamia, 1
MeToo, 58, 60
Michigan, 5, 8, 11, 12, 73, 92, 124,
   132
Microsoft, 33
Middle East, 67, 77, 84
Mike Pence, 99
Milo Yiannopoulos, 93
Minnesota, 8, 65, 66, 124
Mojo Burrito, 44, 94
Muslim ban, 76

N

Namibia, 78
Nancy Pelosi, 74
National Center on Sexual
   Exploitation, 60, 61
National Rifle Association, 68, 70,
   77, 130
Nazis, 44, 94, 125
NBA, 66
NBCUniversal, 84, 85
Nestle, 64, 65, 73, 127
Netflix, 84, 85, 119, 129
New Orleans Saints, 83
Newt Gingrich, 48
Nigel Farage, 71, 72, 122
   Farage, 72, 129
Nike, 9, 29, 34, 65, 79, 80, 81, 82,
   83, 89, 100, 109, 110, 116, 118,
   122, 123, 124, 126, 127, 130
Nordstrom, 97, 119
Noreena Hertz, 34
   Hertz, 34, 77, 124
North America, 1, 29, 58, 71, 103,
   119
North Korea, 113
NRA, 65, 68, 69, 70, 72, 77, 122, 128

O

Obergefell v. Hodges, 8

P

PAC, 6, 26
PACs, viii, 6, 11, 49, 50, 120
Patagonia, 44, 62, 119, 128
Peloton, 87, 88, 120, 121, 123, 125, 128
Pepsi, 30, 59, 131
Pfizer, 40
Phillip Morris, 29
Pierre-Yves Neron, 16, 26
    Neron, 26, 27, 127
Playboy Group, 6
political conflict system, 16
Prada, 84
public choice theory, 50

Q

Qantas, 53

R

racism, vi, 44, 55, 92, 94, 107
Red Hen, 98, 99, 120
Reebok, 34, 116
REI, 44, 119
Republican Party, 7, 10, 41, 48, 49, 50, 65, 67, 70, 84, 85, 91, 92, 97, 100, 118
Republicans, 48, 49, 50, 70, 74, 100, 128
Robert Clive, 2
Roe v. *Wade*, 24
Rome, 1

Ronald Coase, viii, 1
Ronald Reagan, 7, 24
Roscoe Conkling
    Conkling, 21, 22, 23
Roseanne Barr, 92
Russia, 78
Rutherford B. Hayes, 2
Ryan Reynolds, 88, 121

S

Salesforce, 33, 35, 125
Salvation Army, 64
same-sex couples, 62, 67
Samuel P. Huntington, 116, 121
San Francisco, 35, 121
Sanofi, 92, 127
Sarah Huckabee Sanders, 98
Scotland, 72
seller's market, 15
sexism, vi, 35, 55, 58, 87, 107
Shell, 27
Sidney & Beatrice Webb, 43
Silicon Valley, 3, 94, 97
single-issue, 49, 53
Sleeping Giants, 74, 86
South African, 57
South America, 28
Southern Pacific Railroad, 21, 22
Soviet Union, 3
Stacy Abrams, 84
Starbucks, 108, 119
Stephen J. Field, 22
Stoneman Douglas, 69, 70, 76
Sumer, vi, 1

T

Taco Bell, 117

Taiwan, 105, 106, 107, 109, 119,
   124
Target, 63, 65, 66, 68, 124, 127
Tehran, 61
The Dollar Shave Club, 89
Thomas Hobbes, 38, 124
Tibet, 105, 106, 119, 124
Tiffany's, 78, 79, 89
Tim Cook, 109, 124
Tim Gionet, 93
Time Warner, 97
Tom Emmer, 65
Tommy Robison, 72
Top Dog, 44
transgender, 62, 66
TripAdvisor, 73
Tucker Carlson, 93
Twitter, vi, 57, 72, 91, 92, 93, 94, 95,
   98, 120, 123, 125, 130

U

Uber, 76
Undercover, 109
United Airlines, 54
United Kingdom, 33, 61, 63, 71
United Nations, 77
United States Supreme Court, v,
   viii, 7, 10, 13, 16, 27, 38, 45, 75

V

Vans, 109, 110, 129, 132
Versace, 103, 106, 129

Vietnam, 45, 79
Vietnam War, 45
Virginia Company, 2
Voxpro, 66

W

Wal-Mart, 60, 61, 62, 73, 86, 114,
   118, 120, 131
WarnerMedia, 84, 85, 119, 129
Wayfair, 73
Weibo, 106
Wendy's, 117
West Indies, 2
Western Europe, 1, 28
Women's Day, 54, 55, 56, 120
World Bank, 67, 103, 131
World Health Organization, 65

X

Xiaomi, 108

Y

Yves Saint Lauren, 84

Z

Zara, 107
zoon politikon, 37, 50

www.ingramcontent.com/pod-product-compliance
Lightning Source LLC
Chambersburg PA
CBHW071132280326
41935CB00010B/1197